TOWARDS OPEN SKIES AND
UNCONGESTED AIRPORTS

The Hong Kong Centre for Economic Research

The Hong Kong Centre for Economic Research
The Chinese University of Hong Kong
Shatin, Hong Kong
Tel: 0-6042424   Fax: 852-0-6954234

TOWARDS OPEN SKIES AND UNCONGESTED AIRPORTS

An Opportunity for Hong Kong

Kai-sun Kwong

Published for

The Hong Kong Centre for Economic Research

by

The Chinese University Press

ISBN 962-201-442-9

THE CHINESE UNIVERSITY PRESS
The Chinese University of Hong Kong
SHATIN, N. T., HONG KONG

Printed in Hong Kong by Polydesign Printing Co., Ltd.

To

My Parents, Kwong-Lee and Oi-Mi

and

My Wife, Teresa.

Contents

List of Tables

Foreword

The HKCER Paperbacks are planned to be studies of medium length in which economists would analyse the relationship between theory and policy. Authors are invited, in particular, to consider the circumstances which encouraged or inhibited the translation of ideas into policy.

This Paperback traces the development of the international airline industry, analyses its structure, points out the problems which inhibit maximum economic efficiency, and suggest policies which would improve the best interests of the travelling public.

Dr. Kwong draws important lessons from two relevant observations. First, deregulation of the U.S. domestic airline industry has made its costs and fares lower than they otherwise would have been, while services have become more frequent. Airports have become more congested as a consequence. Nevertheless, travellers have benefited enormously from more competition among airlines. Dr. Kwong argues that there is no compelling reason why international travellers cannot enjoy similar benefits if the international airline industry were to be liberalized.

Second, despite obvious benefits to most travellers and some airlines, it is difficult to liberalize the international airline industry because multilateral open-sky agreements are too costly to negotiate and conclude. An alternative which requires governments to negotiate bilateral open-sky agreements is proposed. Dr. Kwong shows, using Hong Kong as an example, how even modest breakthroughs at the beginning could create incentives for more countries to seek bilateral open-sky agreements with each other; as the momentum gathers, it could in time lead to liberalization on a global scale.

Hong Kong appears to be a natural place to adopt a bilateral open-sky policy. It has a free market tradition whose reputation can only be enhanced by liberalization; as a major hub and an international city located in the fastest growing region in Asia it stands to benefit more from liberalization; its airlines are highly efficient and may benefit from a more open system. Dr. Kwong urges Hong Kong to adopt such a policy for its own benefit. He further proposes a scheme to auction landing time slots to reduce airport congestion, a problem which gains urgency with liberalization.

The international airline industry has developed at a spectacular rate since World War II and is now one of the fastest growing and most technologically advanced of all world industries. In the coming years, there will be major shifts in global demand patterns. An industry regulated by rules devised more that four decades ago and designed to limit free competition will appear increasingly inadequate. Reforming the system will not be easy, some would tell us that it is impossible and others would have us believe that we already have the best of all possible worlds. Dr. Kwong has helped us to focus on the crucial issues in a highly complex industry and has proposed a surprisingly simple scheme to liberalize the industry and reduce airport congestion. He does not pretend to be able to foresee all the consequences of liberalization, but argues convincingly that it would be in the interest of the consumers.

The Trustees, Advisers, and Director of the Hong Kong Centre for Economic Research, must formally dissociate themselves from the conclusions of the Paperback, while welcoming its contribution to an issue that is topical and becoming increasingly urgent.

Richard Y.C. Wong
August 1988

The Author

Dr. Kai-sun Kwong obtained his Bachelor of Social Science degree in Economics and Management Studies with First Class Honours from the University of Hong Kong. He was awarded a Commonwealth Scholarship to pursue graduate studies in economics at the University of British Columbia in Canada. He is at present Lecturer in the Department of Economics at The Chinese University of Hong Kong.

Dr. Kwong specializes in consumer theory, social choice and welfare economics. He has published academic papers concerning taxation, inequality measurement and voting systems. His current research interests include, deregulation of industries, allocation mechanisms through auctioning and axiomatic assessment of social choice rules.

Acknowledgment

I would like to thank Daniel Gressel for his stimulating conversation and Richard Y.C. Wong for his enthusiastic support and discussion throughout the project. I am most grateful to Sir Alan Peacock for his reading through an earlier draft and offering me many constructive comments. James Foster, Peter Heady, Clyde McAvoy and Richard Stirland, all airline experts, have offered me valuable information about the industry. Thanks are also due to Barbara Boozer for vastly improving my presentation, Eliza Chan for typing several drafts of the manuscript, and P.K. Wong for his computational assistance. Finally, I wish to express my gratitude to the Hong Kong Centre for Economic Research for making the project feasible.

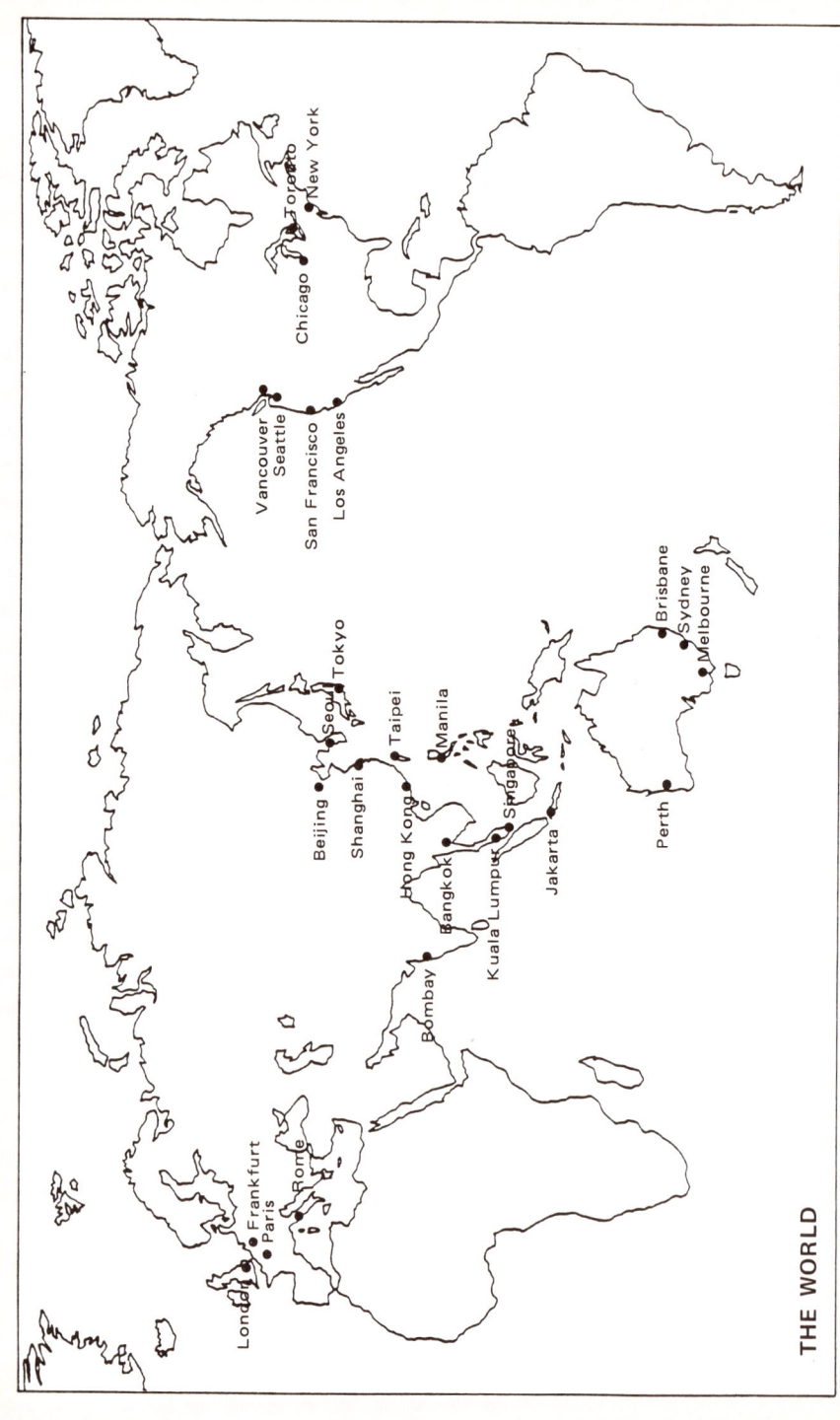

THE WORLD

1 Introduction

All major cities of the world face two difficult questions in connection with the airline industry:

(1) How can the international airline industry be rationalized given the fact that landing rights are tightly bound by international agreements?

(2) How can the airport be better managed to ease congestion in view of the fact that major capacity expansion cannot immediately keep pace with growth in demand for services?

This book addresses both questions and proposes solutions for both problems. Although the proposals are based on the Hong Kong context and are addressed to the Hong Kong public, they could have worldwide impact if they were converted into policies. Indeed it is argued that global liberalization has a better chance of succeeding if one country proposes to go ahead first, rather than waiting for the conclusion of multilateral negotiations.

The international airline industry is heavily regulated.[1] This means the airlines are not free to enter any market, to determine the number of flights on a certain route, and to set their own airfares. Route changes and additions are matters to be concluded through negotiation with foreign government bureaucrats and politicians. Permission is granted in light of the impact that it would have on the country's own airlines.

Airfare changes are subject to the approval of airlines that operate the same route through collusive agreements and in some

---

[1] Charter flights which account for about 3% of passenger volume in Hong Kong are ignored.

cases, business cartels such as International Air Transport Association (IATA) and the Orient Airlines Association (OAA). A right to land is a jealously guarded privilege that no government is willing to confer unless compensation in the form of reciprocal rights or diplomatic advantages is available. Fearing that granting landing rights to more foreign airlines would expose the country's own airlines to competitive pressure, governments actively bar foreign airlines from landing their planes. One undesirable result is that passengers have to pay more than necessary. Chapter 2 highlights the historical development of the industry and its present undesirable state. The deregulation of the U.S. domestic airline industry illustrates the benefits that one can expect from a deregulated airline industry. It is argued that similar benefits would likely be gained from a liberalized international airline industry.

As in other countries, the Hong Kong Government at present controls the routes of Hong Kong airlines. The fight over Chinese air routes between Cathay Pacific and Dragonair is worth mentioning. Apparently, the government favours the present situation where scheduled air routes between Hong Kong and key cities in China are monopolized by Cathay Pacific and the Civil Aviation Administration of China. Despite repeated strong protests, Dragonair has been unable to obtain rights to fly many Chinese routes on a scheduled basis. The government has adopted a "one-route-one-airline" policy. It claims that if along a certain route one airline already offers adequate service, two airlines would create excess capacity so that neither could make a profit and, as a result, the consumer would suffer from deterioration of service. In the midst of the struggle, Cathay Pacific continually reported healthy profits and Dragonair dismal losses.[2] How should the government handle this matter in future?

---

[2] With respect to Hong Kong, Cathay Pacific accounted for 3,695,547 passenger movements while Dragonair accounted for a mere 59,087 passenger movements from April 1986 to March 1987.

Under the present regulatory framework, Dragonair knows that a route once granted is unlikely to be taken away. Potential competitors are discouraged from seeking entry. It is the future reward from the right to operate certain routes that keeps Dragonair in the industry despite losses. In the U.S., before deregulation, all domestic air routes were granted by the Civil Aeronautics Board (CAB). CAB received more applications for route rights than it could handle.[3] The airlines' real intention was to pre-empt the entry of rival airlines and to keep a high profile in the industry.

It is proposed here that what the government could do is to open up the air routes, not only to Dragonair, but to all future airlines of Hong Kong. The Hong Kong Government should conclude bilateral agreements with other countries that would permit free entry for their airlines on routes between them. This would allow the two Hong Kong airlines to expand services on these routes. Chapter 3 introduces a Sequential Bilateral Liberalization scheme which calls for the Hong Kong Government to open up markets with eight countries. It is argued that the U.S., Japan, Taiwan, Thailand, Singapore, the U.K., Australia and Malaysia should be approached for bilateral liberalization. If liberalization with these countries was successful, the other countries would follow. Eventually, those countries would in turn open up their markets among themselves.

An airport is an important asset to a city. It provides communication links for passengers, mail and cargo. In modern society, an airport is a prerequisite to development of trade, foreign investment and tourism. The importance of an airport is well recognized in Hong Kong. Hong Kong's Kai Tak Airport has undergone several stages of expansion. However, the growth in demand for airline services has prevented the congestion problem from being solved. The possibility of a new airport being built as a long-term solution is now being considered. In the

---

[3] See Bailey *et al.* (1985) Chapter 4.

short-term, the crux of the problem is really inefficiency in airport management because airport services are not priced to reflect their scarcity value.

Although the airport departure tax (HK$100) is among the highest in the world, it does not ease congestion because it is levied uniformly on all passengers.[4] It is difficult to view the tax as anything other than an easy source of revenue. Since Kai Tak Airport terminal suffers from a peak load problem, i.e., saturation of capacity during peak hours but under-utilization during off-peak hours, Chapter 4 proposes a scheme which would require the airlines to pay an amount that reflects the value of airport facilities at the time of use. In practice, airlines would be asked to bid for landing time slots. It is argued that an auctioning scheme for landing time slots would not only be economically sensible, but also practically feasible. The administrative problems could be solved.

The auctioning of airport time slots and the liberalization of the industry are two interconnected issues. Firstly, foreign countries might not be willing to liberalize with Hong Kong if they are barred from landing their planes in the more desired time slots. Auctioning is a mechanism that would permit the allocation of such time slots to the airline which values them most. Secondly, without liberalization, airfares might be too rigid so that airlines occupying the heavily demanded slots might be reluctant to accept auctioning which would increase their costs but not their revenues. For this reason, liberalization should come before time slot auctioning. Thirdly, after liberalization, traffic through the Hong Kong airport would increase rapidly. Auctioning time slots would ensure efficient and equitable allocation of airport resources among the airlines and travellers. In summary, auctioning and liberalization are integral parts of one coherent scheme rather than two separate policy proposals.

---

[4] The airport departure tax has been reduced from HK$120 to HK$100 as from April 1, 1988. The tax has no apparent effect in reducing passenger volume.

The demand for airline services is expected to grow at a pace that a rigidly regulated industry cannot efficiently cope with. The problem is likely to be particularly acute in Asia. A larger share of the global income is gradually being shifted to the Asian countries, which are eagerly looking outwards for investment outlets and cheaper production sites. The advancement in telecommunications technology has facilitated control of overseas ventures. The two largest communist countries, China and the Soviet Union, are experimenting with reforms that may open up their economic and political systems. This may be a major impetus to regional and international development. As more and more people travel abroad, the tourist industry will become further developed. All these factors point to fast growth in the demand for airline services. In the foreseeable future, for long-distance travel, there will be no substitute for travelling by plane. The time is right for governments of the world to liberalize the international airline industry in order to meet this growth in demand.

On the production side, civil aviation technology is very much standardized. International airlines use the same planes, the same fuel and the same airports. Cost variations are mainly attributable to differences in wage costs and management efficiency. If the market is allowed to work freely, costs tend to equalize and prices tend to fall. Liberalization would greatly benefit consumers. It is widely recognized that free trade is a superior alternative to protected trade.

This book develops the argument that Hong Kong can initiate policies which would eventually lead to global liberalization of the airline industry. It should be emphasized that liberalization of the industry would bring significant benefits not only to the world but also for Hong Kong. The travelling public would enjoy lower airfares, more choice of service, and more convenient flights. The general public would gain from the spillover effects that result from the business boom in hotels, restaurants and retail trade. The two Hong Kong airlines could take advantage of the growth opportunities that liberalization would bring. Hong Kong would further establish itself as an international centre and enhance its reputation as a free-port. These benefits would be captured if the Hong Kong Government succeeds in implementing a policy of bilateral liberalization with other countries. It is worth mentioning that these benefits would accrue to Hong Kong even before full global liberalization of the international airline industry is accomplished.

2 The International Airline Industry: Regulation and Liberalization

Historical Background

During the first few years of the twentieth century, the feasibility of the airplane was demonstrated by the Wright Brothers. Although airplanes were used during the First World War, however, regular passenger service did not start until 1919. On the one hand, airplanes were like sealiners in providing domestic and international transportation of passengers and cargo. On the other hand, increasing use of airplanes created unique problems. Western countries realized the importance of airplanes to national security and passenger safety. Consequently, the Convention for the Regulation of Aerial Navigation was held in Paris in 1919. The major agreement achieved was that each country had sovereign control over the air space above the country's territory. The next important event in aviation history was the Convention for the Unification of Certain Rules regarding International Air Transport held in Warsaw in 1929. Some technical matters were settled including liabilities of carriers, documentation of carriage and other conditions of travel.

By 1940, the potential of the air transportation industry was well recognized, however, there was no agreement on the conditions of granting air routes and landing rights. These issues were seen to have far reaching economic impact on Western countries. The convention held in Chicago in 1944 was an attempt to address these issues and to arrive at some sort of agreement. Fifty-four nations participated in the convention to promote air traffic. The crucial outcome of the Chicago Convention was the signing of the multilateral International Air Services Transit Agreement which allowed passenger planes to fly through sovereign air space and land for refueling and other technical reasons. At the convention, some countries (led by the U.S.) advocated free entry to all air routes while some other countries (led by the U.K.) favoured strict control over routes and capacity. The regulationists feared that open competition would bring disastrous results and jeopardize the growth of the industry. They also feared that the U.S., with its military and financial strength, would eventually dominate the industry. All sorts of proposals were voiced, however, no agreement was reached.[1]

With multilateral agreement having been proved unfeasible, the two powers of the industry, namely the U.S. and the U.K., negotiated bilaterally and the outcome was the Bermuda Agreement signed in February, 1946. The agreement set up a model of agreement which was subsequently followed by other countries in similar bilateral agreements. It also started a fare-fixing body, the International Air Transport Association (IATA), which still persists today.

The Bermuda Agreement marked the retreat of both the U.S. and the U.K. from their respective aviation policy positions. The U.K. relaxed their rigid stand on capacity restriction and the U.S. theirs on free market pricing. From the agreement, five "freedoms" emerged. The first freedom refers to the right of a plane of a contracting party to fly across the air space of the other without landing. The second freedom refers to the right to land for technical reasons. The first and second freedoms were actually agreed upon at the Chicago Convention. The third freedom refers to the right of a plane of a contracting party to deliver passengers, mail and cargo taken up in the territory to the other country. The fourth freedom is the reverse of the third freedom, i.e., it is the right to take up passengers, mail and cargo from the other country and deliver them to the territory. The fifth freedom is the right to pick up foreign passengers and deliver them in another foreign country. After the Bermuda Agreement was signed

---

[1] See Chuang (1972) chapters 1 and 2 for details.

between the U.S. and the U.K., other countries soon followed the model and signed bilateral agreements among themselves. Bilateral agreements were obviously much easier to achieve than the multilateral agreements attempted at the Chicago Convention.

According to the agreement, no capacity restriction is placed on third and fourth freedom traffic but capacity for fifth freedom traffic is implicitly restricted by perceived demand arising from on-route countries. The rather imprecise language left much room for on-route countries to restrict fifth freedom traffic. For example, a direct flight from Hong Kong to Singapore by Cathay Pacific is allowed by the third freedom and from Singapore to Hong Kong by the fourth freedom. Now consider a stop in a third country, say Bangkok, Thailand. A Hongkong-Bangkok-Singapore flight would involve (in addition to the third and fourth freedoms between Hong Kong and Singapore) the fifth freedom in the Bangkok-Singapore leg. If Bangkok does not generate sufficient traffic, Thailand may restrict the capacity of the route.

Allowing the five freedoms for air routes represented an effort to compromise on the part of the U.K. and, in return, the U.S. agreed to the machinery of IATA to settle airfares subject to government approval. Simply put, IATA was a business cartel that comprised most of the major airlines of the free world. Airfare conferences were held to settle airfares subject to the agreement of all airlines concerned. The airlines then submitted the determined airfares to their respective governments for approval. In the fare-fixing process, complex rules were followed which stipulated, for example, that airfares for indirect flights between points A and B must not be cheaper than direct flights between A and B. IATA also took action to discipline airlines if they tried to undercut fixed prices. Airlines that deviated from rules were liable to fines. Over the years, many airlines have been fined possibly because fines were not prohibitive although details are not disclosed. In any case, cartelized price control was seen by the U.K. in 1946 as an effective means to prevent the U.S. from dominating the industry by undercutting the airfares of European airlines.

After the Bermuda Agreement, the U.S. held a very liberal position towards granting fifth freedom route rights partly because of its own free-market standpoint and partly because it saw other airlines as no threat to the dominating U.S. airlines. From 1950 onwards, the growth of the industry slackened and the expansion of fifth freedom routes that took advantage of the U.S. prompted the U.S. government to be more cautious. Since then, the industry was plagued by more and more regulations in terms of route grants, capacity restrictions and fare-setting.

Present State of the Industry

Many factors led to increasingly protectionist attitudes after 1950. Slackened growth merely prompted awareness of them.

Countries were increasingly aware of the uneven benefits for two countries that granted each other fifth freedom flights. For example, Japan Air Lines negotiated with the U.S. for fifth freedom flights beyond New York to Europe in the sixties. The North Atlantic routes were the most lucrative. In exchange, U.S. airlines could have fifth freedom flights beyond Tokyo and Osaka. Obviously, Japan Air Lines derived a great deal of benefit from the deal. To counter uneven benefits, which to a large extent were due to geographical locations, governments felt they had to impose capacity restrictions.

Another category of routes gradually developed, which were known informally as sixth freedom routes. The sixth freedom arises from combining two third/fourth freedom routes. Exact classification of sixth freedom routes remains in dispute today as exemplified by the following case which occurred recently between the U.K. and Malaysia. At present, Malaysian Air Systems maintains several Australia-Malaysia flights and several Malaysia-U.K. flights.[2] Flight MH4A is Sydney-Melbourne-

---

[2] Flight details are extracted from ABC World Airways Guide.

Kuala Lumpur, which arrives in Kuala Lumpur at 20:35. Flight MH4 is Kuala Lumpur-Dubai-Amsterdam-London which departs Kuala Lumpur at 23:15. The U.K. Government argued that MH4 in conjunction with MH4A is invading the Australia-London markets although the two flights separately only exercise the fourth and third freedoms between Malaysia and Australia, and between Malaysia and the U.K. The U.K. Government refused to grant more flights of the same kind as MH4 on these grounds. Malaysia bitterly opposed the decision. Actually, examples of sixth freedom flight are abundant in history. In the sixties, Royal Dutch KLM maintained a New York-Amsterdam-Paris flight, which the U.S. Government alleged was invading the New York-Paris market. Sixth freedom opportunities are thus another reason for governments to restrict even third and fourth freedom traffic capacity.

The principle of the Bermuda Agreement of allowing unlimited capacity in third and fourth freedom traffic has gradually faded. Capacity restriction takes many forms in practice. One form is to specify the particular type of aircraft that can be used to fly a route. Another form, which is more common today, is to specify the frequency of flights along a route. In most cases, the exact route, including all the stopover points, must be specified in route applications. In many bilateral air services agreements, the countries' airlines are allowed to negotiate the airfare structure. All the regulations combine to shape an industry in which airlines cannot compete in terms of price, service or route pattern.

Any system that has persisted for so long must yield gains to some of the parties involved, otherwise the interested parties would have come together to change it. Three interest groups can be identified that are related to the aviation industry, namely, airline management, aircraft manufacturers, and passengers—with a possible fourth group, the governments.[3]

---

[3] The political economy of the industry is discussed in Straszheim (1969), chapters 1 and 2.

A government may try to represent the interests of passengers on one hand, and protect the airlines and aircraft manufacturers on the other. Imposing regulations on the industry is a manifestation of a protectionist attitude towards airlines and aircraft manufacturers at the expense of passengers, who would favour a free industry and lower airfares. Based on economic considerations alone, a country need not have its own airline, although most countries do. To keep the flag carriers viable, the governments impose regulations to hinder competition and, as a last resort, subsidize the airline. The passengers who lose under regulation are too diffused to protest collectively.

Reasons have been cited, from the government point of view, for supporting an airline. It is believed that an airline earns foreign exchange and improves the balance of payments, although there exist better alternatives that yield the same benefit. Some governments believe that an airline is essential to promote tourism and foreign investment, although other more efficient airlines appear willing to meet increased traffic demand if it arises. There are other reasons that have been cited in the past but do not seem to apply anymore. It was believed that to promote development in colonies and facilitate control over them, an airline was necessary to operate flights even if they were not profitable. Most of these colonies have gained independence since then and few are left today. It used to be the case that, for military purposes, countries felt the need to support the aircraft industry and to deploy passenger planes in times of war. The civil aircraft industry today is dominated by the U.S. companies. The same applies increasingly to the military aircraft industry at a time when unified defense and more cooperation between North Atlantic countries is favoured. The conclusion is that at present there seems to be little basis to justify the governments' protectionist attitude towards airlines besides the intangible and illusory one of maintaining national prestige.

If a government has no real reason for protecting its airlines, the passengers stand to gain in a free market, and there is no need to support any infant aircraft industry anywhere, what is preventing the aviation industry from being rationalized? The answer lies in the airlines themselves and, to the extent that many airlines are partly government-owned, in the governments as well. Airlines are not equally efficient. European airlines have to bear higher wage costs and higher fuel costs than U.S. airlines. Asian airlines are famous for their hospitable service, new planes and attractive stopover packages. On the other hand, some third world airlines have to bear very high capital costs. Despite capacity and route restrictions, governments are unable to equate profitability across airlines. Some governments have to subsidize their flag carriers. The problem is, once an airline is protected and then subsidized, the management has no incentive to change and improve. Behind the walls of protection, workers also wish to keep their high wage rates and short working hours. Since the management and the workers are the best organized interest groups, and the government is content with a modest level of service, there is no real pressure to fully expose the airline to foreign competition.

Deregulation of the Domestic U.S. Airlines

In 1978, there was a major policy change in the U.S. domestic airline industry.[4] Although the strategy used there does not apply directly to the international airline industry, some lessons can be learned.

For two decades after 1949, the domestic industry of the U.S. enjoyed an average annual growth of 14%. The Civil Aeronautics Board (CAB), an arm of the government, regulated the industry heavily. The CAB structured routes and determined flight frequencies according to perceived passenger demand. Scheduled operators were neither allowed to enter markets nor to leave them. While airfares were not individually determined, the

---

4 Consult Bailey *et al.* (1985) for the transition of the industry during deregulation. For a recent assessment, see Kahn (1988).

CAB imposed a ceiling on the percentage of profits on stockholder equity. As a consequence, airlines tended to adjust airfares in unison, which, because of regulated capacity, had little relationship with costs.

Three factors led to the eventual deregulation of the industry. Firstly, it was realized that the rigid route pattern could not cope with the rapid growth in demand for transportation. Secondly, there was much cross-subsidization between routes since airlines were compelled to fly unprofitable routes and competition was barred in the profitable ones. This led to a serious argument about fairness. Thirdly, there emerged small intrastate carriers which offered very low airfares as they were outside the jurisdiction of the CAB. Moreover, these small carriers were apparently very profitable. The public became increasingly aware of these factors, and the Airline Deregulation Act was signed into law in October, 1978 by President Carter.

The Deregulation Act had a widespread impact on the industry. Its effects are grouped under five headings, as discussed below.

(i) Airfare Structure

Under deregulation, new entrants into markets compete with incumbents by undercutting existing prices. The general airfare level has been lower since deregulation. There has been more widespread use of discounts, often with restrictions, e.g., advance purchase and minimum stay requirements. Price discrimination has been increasingly used, i.e., charging different passengers different airfares for the same flight to capture price-conscious passengers. Peak-load pricing, i.e., charging higher prices in times of heavy demand, is also possible as a result of pricing freedom. In close connection with the change in airfare structure is the change in service varieties. Under deregulation, airlines can offer a large variety of flight classes which differ in the quality of services provided as a means of price discrimination and market segmentation. The result is an increase in the utilization rate of planes and a decrease in cost.

(ii) Route Structure

The most significant change to route structure since deregulation has been the emergence of the so-called "hub-and-spoke" system. Airlines establish strong bases at the hubs—such as New York, Chicago and Los Angeles—and bring passengers from the smaller nearby centres to the hubs by short flights. The passengers then transfer to another flight on a major route for another hub, where, in case this is not their final destination, they transfer to another short feeder flight. From society's point of view, this route pattern (which has evolved by itself since deregulation) is more efficient than the diffused and complex network that the CAB tried to maintain before deregulation, in which even small centres were linked by direct flights.[5] This pattern has also increased the utilization rate of airplanes as capacity can now be adjusted to suit the size of passenger demand in different markets. Smaller planes can be used for feeder traffic and large ones for trunk routes.

(iii) Quality of Service

As a result of competition from new entrants, low-quality-low-price flights are offered. This represents for the most part, an enriched variety of choice. The passenger who is more concerned with price than comfort benefits greatly. But the passenger who is willing to pay the full-coach airfare charged before deregulation might find it less available. He could, of course, choose a business class seat, however, since deregulation the planes are much more congested and direct flights are fewer. This passenger, who is in the minority, has done worse under deregulation.

---

5 For a rigorous discussion, see Morrison and Winston (1985).

(iv) Congestion

Since deregulation, congestion has increased in planes as well as in airports. Congestion in planes is a result of efforts to increase plane utilization rates and price discrimination. Congestion at airports is the result of the large number of budget travellers who are taking advantage of lower airfares. But congestion cannot really be viewed as a drawback of deregulation. The fall in quality of air service has been compensated for by the fall in price. Actually, delays at airports are attributable to the inability of the government to manage and expand the airports efficiently to cope with increased traffic rather than to the inefficiency of airlines.

(v) Concentration

It was widely believed prior to deregulation that if free entry to all markets were permitted, a large number of airlines would co-exist and compete against each other, ensuring the lowest airfare to the passengers. While it is true that airfares are cheaper and more price-quality options are available, the concentration of the industry has produced some unexpected twists.

Immediately after deregulation, many small airlines invaded new markets as expected. Since the beginning of the 1980s, almost all of them have disappeared, partly because of the rise in oil prices (which led to cost escalations and economic recession) and partly because of overly-aggressive management style. Moreover, big airlines had clear advantages over smaller ones. They were able to undercut rivals financially. They maintained an extensive network with strong operation bases at the hubs and so were able to offer convenient transfers and same-airline discounts. Advances in computer technology also gave them some monopolistic power through the reservation systems.[6] Lastly, the frequent-flyer discount programs proved attractive to travellers.

---

[6] See Fisher (1987) for reasons of monopoly over the computer reservation system.

Although deregulation has not reduced concentration, the fact that airlines can enter any market freely does mean that airlines cannot charge a price that is substantially above cost. Actually, the number of airlines in each city-pair market did go up after deregulation and, on the basis of price and cost information, there is no evidence suggesting collusion among the airlines to monopolize the industry.

The Effects of Liberalizing the International Industry

The question of how to liberalize the industry receives full treatment in the next chapter. Our concern here is what we can expect from a liberalized international airline industry.

Admittedly the impact of liberalization would be so extensive that only some of the consequences can be predicted here. The U.S. deregulation policy has brought a few surprises to economists and we are fortunate in being able to draw on their experience in making our predictions. The multi-dimensional effects are grouped under five headings for discussion.

(i) Airfares

Our first concern is the movement of airfares after liberalization. Table 1 shows a comparison of present airfares for some major routes in the global network. North America, Asia and Europe are treated separately and, in each area, domestic and international flights are distinguished.[7] The basis of comparison is price (in U.S. dollars) per kilometer for one-way flights.[8] A few observations can be readily made. Firstly, the structure of airfares is

---

[7] The city-pairs are selected based on distance and expected traffic volume.

[8] Prices which are expressed originally in local currencies are taken from ABC World Airways Guide. Price comparisons are much affected by the recent wide swings in exchange rates.

Table 1
Economy Class Airfare Comparison (January 1988)
(in U.S. Dollars per kilometre)

Km.	NORTH AMERICA		ASIA		EUROPE	
	Domestic	Int'l	Domestic	Int'l	Domestic	Int'l
0-500	Chicago-Detroit (384 Km) 0.34-0.51 min=0.08	Montreal-Boston (446 Km) 0.14-0.17 min=0.13	Penang-Kuala Lumpur (315 Km) 0.07-0.11	Singapore-Kuala Lumpur (300 Km) 0.21	London-Leeds (480 Km) 0.08-0.25	Geneva-Paris (480 Km) 0.39
501-1000	New York-Detroit (777 Km) 0.19-0.29 min=0.14	Toronto-Washington (576 Km) 0.19-0.28 min=0.19	Bangkok-Chiangmai (620 Km) 0.07-0.08	Hongkong-Taipei (900 Km) 0.15	Hamburg-Munich (930 Km) 0.21	London-Frankfurt (960 Km) 0.08
1001-1500	Los Angeles Denver (1340 Km) 0.08-0.22 min=0.08	Vancouver-San Fran. (1370 Km) 0.10-0.13 min=0.10	Tokyo-Fukuoka (1155 Km) 0.16	Singapore-Bangkok (1431 Km) 0.17	London-Aberdeen (1140 Km) 0.07-0.12	London-Vienna (1500 Km) 0.22-0.25
1501-2000	Denver-Detroit (1865 Km) 0.10-0.18 min=0.10	Vancouver-Los Angeles (1800 Km) 0.09-0.12 min=0.09	---	Hongkong-Bangkok (1800 Km) 0.11	---	Frankfurt-Lisbon (2000 Km) 0.26
2001-2500	New York-Dallas (2216 Km) 0.07-0.18 min=0.07	Toronto-Houston (2106 Km) 0.10-0.12 min=0.10	---	Taipei-Tokyo (2400 Km) 0.13	---	London-Athens (2800 Km) 0.06-0.17
over 2500	San Fran.-New York (4147 Km) 0.08-0.13 min=0.08	Toronto-Los Angeles (3500 Km) 0.08-0.11 min=0.08	---	Hongkong-Tokyo (3200 Km) 0.09	---	Stockholm-Lisbon (3596 Km) 0.20

Notes: 1. The "min" unit price refers to the cheapest airfare class available.
2. Exchange Rates:
1 US Dollar = 1.202 Canadian Dollar = 7.8 HK Dollar = 130.65 Japanese Yen
= 2.591 Malaysian Ringgit = 2.042 Singaporean Dollar = 0.578 British Pound
= 1.816 Deutsche Mark = 28.889 Taiwanese Dollar = 24.762 Thai Baht.

Source: ABC World Airways Guide, Hammond Almanac, Cathay Pacific Route Maps, and Rand McNally Road Atlas.

complex and not systematic; however, there is no evidence that airfares are related to airline costs. Secondly, in all areas, generally speaking, international flights seem to be more expensive than domestic flights. Although the sample is small and a definitive conclusion cannot be drawn yet, that this is true should surprise nobody. In North America, deregulation has lowered the general level of airfares and has resulted in a large variety of price-quality combinations. The figures in Table 1 show the range of prices in domestic U.S. flights.[9] In Asia and Europe, there is cross-subsidization. For political reasons, domestic flights are subsidized by profits obtained from international flights. Thirdly, contrary to the common belief that, on a per kilometer basis, "the longer the flight, the cheaper it is", our figures show that no clear pattern emerges in support of this belief. Major factors that determine airfares may include traffic volume, load factors, degrees of competition from rival airlines, amount of subsidy due to political factors and discretionary pricing. Fourthly, comparing across areas, airfares seem to be highest in Europe, lower in Asia and lowest in North America. European airfares are high partly because fuel prices and wage rates are high and partly because the airlines are protected from competition.[10] Asian airfares are lower because wage rates are lower (which offsets high fuel prices) and volume of traffic is high. North American airfares are lowest because deregulation has caused general airfares to become lower and price-quality variations to increase, and because of lower fuel prices.

Now, what are the likely effects of liberalization on the airfare structure? One immediate effect would probably be a sharp increase in traffic volume, which would improve utilization rates and allow airlines to capture economies of scale (e.g., better training programs, more skillful management, better ground ser-

---

[9] Unit price ranges refer to economy classes.
[10] See Sawers (1987) and Pryke (1987) for reasons underlying high European airfares.

vice, etc.). Increased volume per se would reduce general airfares. Furthermore, as airlines are free to enter any market, they would compete against each other by offering lower airfares.

On the other hand, given that European airlines incur higher fuel and wage costs which may be difficult to lower, they probably could not compete effectively with North American and Asian airlines.

An expansion of price-quality options might occur in the industry. In addition, for each airline offering cheap "no-frills" flight classes to capture the price-sensitive passengers, some airlines might have to specialize in specific consumer groups. The European airlines might be forced to move up-market in order to specialize in the high-price-high-service-quality market and leave the low-price markets to other airlines.

After liberalization, competitive pressure would fall hardest on the international flights because domestic industries could continue to be protected. The airlines, especially the weaker ones, might suffer reduction in profits on their international flights.

The extent of cross-subsidization would be restricted and domestic airfares could increase in line with market conditions. But this would be desirable because it is better for airfares to reflect economic conditions rather than political favouritism. There is no reason why international travellers should continue to subsidize domestic travellers.

(ii) Concentration

It is possible that, because of differences in geographical location and factor costs, when the international airline industry had fully adjusted to liberalization, some airlines would grow while others would shrink. There would probably be three types of international airlines: a few giant airlines formed by acquisitions and mergers, which would operate the major routes; a number of small airlines that would run the local and feeder routes; and a few airlines that would be kept in the industry by government subsidies in the name of preserving national prestige. This might not be an undesirable outcome. While the giant airlines would probably dominate the industry in terms of volume and would be able to use various marketing strategies (such as same-airline discounts, worldwide computerized reservation, frequent-flyer programs) to maintain a competitive edge, they could not charge prices that were well above costs. Because of free market entry, any airline could undercut prices. In this sense, liberalization would actually restrict the pricing freedom of giant airlines.[11]

The U.S. experience is also reassuring in that although concentration increased after domestic deregulation, the number of airlines available for each city-pair market also increased, which implies more intense competition in favour of the consumers.[12]

(iii) Airport Congestion

The international network has always followed a "hub-and-spoke" pattern. Since liberalization would most likely increase traffic volume, the hubs would become even busier. Whether congestion would become a problem would depend on what measures the governments adopted and how effective they were. The governments of the major hubs are already working on plans for expansion. The problem is that new capacity may not come into use in time to ease congestion. A proposal described in Chapter 4, which recommends auctioning landing time slots to evenly distribute landings and passenger flow, addresses this problem.

---

[11] This is the contestability hypothesis introduced in Demsetz (1968) and reiterated in Bailey (1981). See also Panzar and Willig (1977) and Posner (1974).
[12] See Kahn (1988).

(iv) *Quality of Service*

There are three aspects to the change in quality of service that could be expected after liberalization.

If governments could not cope with increased passengers at the airports, quality of service would deteriorate significantly. If a particular airport was widely known to be severely congested at a certain time, passengers might avoid flights that landed at peak hours or, if possible, avoid the airport altogether. Airlines might then follow and switch to other airports. Of course, this self-regulating mechanism would be no replacement for better airport management in the short-term and capacity expansion in the long-term.

Since the volume of traffic is expected to increase after liberalization, the number and frequency of flights serving each route would rise especially along the hub-to-hub routes. Those consumers who booked well in advance of departure date would have more flights to choose from. In this sense, the quality of service would definitely improve.

After liberalization a greater variety of flight classes would almost certainly emerge as the airlines tried to attract consumers of different price-sensitivities by offering them different prices. So, in addition to the present first, economy and, on some flights, business classes, more classes such as student class, vacationer class, and commuter class might be introduced. To increase utilization of the current fleet, more flights might be run in off-peak hours, again targeted at the price-sensitive consumers. Thus the price-service combinations would become much more diverse in order to accommodate the diverse preferences of consumers.

(v) *Business Cartel*

A cartel made up of eleven Asian airlines, named Orient Airlines Association (OAA), was established in Manila in 1976. The OAA regulates and polices airfares. It has been claimed that, as a fare-fixing body, OAA is even more effective than IATA.[13]

Under liberalization, IATA and OAA would cease to function as fare-fixing bodies because airlines could enter any market freely. The present ability of business cartels to fix airfares stems from the airlines' cooperation. If a market is regulated as to flight frequency, carrier type and stopover points, there is not much room left for airlines to innovate in order to gain competitive advantage. A price cut may not even translate into an increase in profits because of capacity restrictions. Under these circumstances, airlines fix prices by negotiation and the business cartels assume the role of monitoring compliance after an agreement has been made. Actually, many airlines have cheated and some have been fined, although it is questionable whether a fine can prevent airlines from cheating again. So even under regulation, the cartels do not seem to be very robust. Under liberalization airlines would have freedom to enter or exit any market, and to increase or decrease the number of flights. There would be no incentive to cooperate on prices as each airline would strive to run an optimal business.

The remaining question is whether the airlines that served a route willingly would collude and behave as if they were collectively a monopoly. In practice, this would be unlikely, as evidenced in the U.S. domestic industry. Logically, the scope for collusion would also be small. Firstly, collusion could not prevent new airlines from entering if the route was profitable. Secondly, under free entry, negotiating to form a cartel is very costly. Thirdly, even if a cartel were formed, each airline in the cartel could cheat by price-cutting through rebates to agencies, discounts to qualified consumers, block selling to tourist agencies and by volume-expansion in the form of charter flights and reroutings. Since there would be many ways to legitimately circumvent the cartel agreement, airlines would have little incentive

---

[13] In Hong Kong, Cathay Pacific is a member of only OAA and Dragonair a member of only IATA.

to collude. The conclusion is, under liberalization, IATA, OAA or any other cartel could neither function as fare-fixing bodies nor as vehicles for the maintenance of collusive agreements. No collusion would be likely after liberalization.

Conclusion

The international airline industry has been characterized by heavy regulation since its very beginning. After a multilateral free entry agreement failed in Chicago in 1944, the U.S. and the U.K. signed the bilateral Bermuda Agreement in 1946. Other countries soon followed. While the Bermuda Agreement already restricted fifth freedom traffic, development since then witnessed an increasing degree of restriction over the third and fourth freedoms as well as the fifth freedom. These capacity restrictions have enabled IATA and subsequently OAA to continue as fare-fixing bodies and inefficient airlines to survive in the industry. Such arrangements have allowed some airline workers and management to gain at the expense of consumers through redistribution of the gains.

Due to the obvious inefficiencies of a regulated industry, the U.S. domestic airline industry was deregulated in 1978. Ten years later, the exercise is judged to be largely successful. It is therefore reasonable to expect similar benefits from a liberalized international industry. Airfares are expected to drop on average in part from the emergence of more budget classes. On the major routes, giant airlines would compete with each other while smaller airlines would operate the shorter feeder routes. The range and quality of service provided would become wider and airports would require urgent expansion. As airfares would move freely, the cartels would no longer fix and monitor them.

The presence of vested interests suggests that it would be naive to believe that governments will start liberalizing even if the benefits of liberalization are fully known. Moreover, consumers, who would be the chief beneficiaries from liberalization, lack the organizing power to force the governments to liberalize. One feasible way to liberalize the industry is to select a hub and start bilateral liberalization with other hubs and centres. The following chapter proposes such a strategy using Hong Kong as the hub.

3   A Liberalization Strategy

Introduction

The international airline industry is a regulated industry. The right to operate flights between any two countries is typically reserved for their own airlines. In aviation terminology, this is known as the third and fourth freedom. The right to operate such flights by an airline of a third country (i.e., the fifth freedom) is severely limited. For example, a Cathay Pacific plane which picks up passengers in Hong Kong and delivers them to Tokyo is exercising its third freedom right. It then exercises its fourth freedom right when it picks up passengers in Tokyo and delivers them to Hong Kong on its return. In exchange for this freedom, Japanese airlines are allowed the same flights. Hong Kong and Japanese airlines therefore share the market between them—the number of flights operated by each country is subject to negotiation. Except for one factor, Japan and Hong Kong are monopolists in the Hongkong-Japan market. That exception can be illustrated by the U.S. airline United, which runs a flight Honolulu-Tokyo-Hongkong. The last leg of the flight, Tokyo-Hongkong, is a fifth freedom flight. Both Japan and Hong Kong would try to protect their airlines by restricting United flights if they began picking up a lot of passengers in Tokyo when heading for Hong Kong and in Hong Kong when heading for Tokyo on the return trip. Because of this strict control over routes, airlines can avoid competition that would result in the inefficient airlines losing business to the efficient ones. The undesirable result is that passengers have to pay more in a regulated industry than in a competitive industry and the inefficiencies of certain airlines are concealed.

Table 2

Market Shares in Third, Fourth Freedom Traffic between Hong Kong and other Major Countries (April 1986 - March 1987)

				passenger times	share %
(1)	Japan — Hongkong	3rd/4th freedom	Japan Air Lines	862,814	52.3
			Japan Asia Airways	9,721	0.6
			Total	872,535	
			Cathay Pacific	776,296	47.1
				1,648,831	100.0
		5th freedom	(United, Northwest)	248,264	
(2)	Taiwan — Hongkong	3rd/4th freedom	China Airlines	673,029	55.7
			Cathay Pacific	536,088	44.3
				1,209,117	100.0
		5th freedom	(Korean, Singapore, Thai)	426,694	
(3)	Thailand — Hongkong	3rd/4th freedom	Thai Airways International	534,675	55.7
			Cathay Pacific	424,763	44.3
				959,438	100.0
		5th freedom	(China Airlines)	245,787	
(4)	Philippines — Hongkong	3rd/4th freedom	Philippine Airlines	349,220	49.1
			Cathay Pacific	361,405	50.9
				710,625	100.0
		5th freedom		0	
(5)	Singapore — Hongkong	3rd/4th freedom	Singapore Airlines	415,585	65.3
			Cathay Pacific	220,405	34.7
				635,990	100.0
		5th freedom	(United, China Airlines)	234,024	
(6)	United States — Hongkong	3rd/4th freedom	Northwest Airlines	226,183	41.6
			United Airlines	283,137	52.1
			Cathay Pacific	34,064	6.3
				543,384	100.0
		5th freedom	(Singapore Airlines)	171,739	
(7)	United Kingdom — Hongkong	3rd/4th freedom	British Airways	148,785	29.4
			British Caledonian Airways	120,469	23.8
			Cathay Pacific	237,274	46.8
				506,528	100.0
		5th freedom		0	
(8)	Australia — Hongkong	3rd/4th freedom	Qantas Airways	224,023	45.6
			Cathay Pacific	267,215	54.4
				419,238	100.0
		5th freedom		0	

Table 2 *(cont'd)*

			passenger times	share %
(9)	South Korea — Hongkong	3rd/4th freedom	Korean Air	190,845	60.0
			Cathay Pacific	127,286	40.0
				318,131	100.0
		5th freedom	(Thai)	45,973	
(10)	Malaysia — Hongkong	3rd/4th freedom	Malaysia Airline System	127,374	57.6
			Cathay Pacific	93,764	42.4
				221,138	100.0
		5th freedom	(China Airlines)	45,468	
(11)	Canada — Hongkong	3rd/4th freedom	Canadian Airlines Int'l	77,827	43.0
			Cathay Pacific	103,370	57.0
				181,197	100.0
		5th freedom		0	
(12)	Germany — Hongkong	3rd/4th freedom	Lufthansa	67,650	40.4
			Cathay Pacific	99,944	59.6
				167,594	100.0
		5th freedom		518	
(13)	Indonesia — Hongkong	3rd/4th freedom	Garuda Indonesian Airways	82,460	56.4
			Cathay Pacific	63,839	43.6
				146,299	100.0
		5th freedom		0	
(14)	Italy — Hongkong	3rd/4th freedom	Alitalia	25,662	40.5
			Cathay Pacific	37,772	59.5
				63,434	100.0
		5th freedom		3,363	
(15)	France — Hongkong	3rd/4th freedom	Air France	31,558	56.4
			Cathay Pacific	24,395	43.6
				55,953	100.0
		5th freedom		0	
(16)	Holland — Hongkong	3rd/4th freedom	KLM Royal Dutch Airlines	22,809	76.6
			Cathay Pacific	6,957	23.4
				29,766	100.0
		5th freedom		0	

Notes: 1. Fifth freedom traffic is often shared by a number of airlines, only the major ones are shown unless otherwise stated.

2. Dragonair has served flights to Japan, Thailand, Indonesia, and Malaysia. Its shares in these markets are all less than 1%.

Source: Report on Civil Aviation Hong Kong 1986 -1987

It is clear why, despite the apparent success of the U.S. experience in deregulating its domestic airline industry, and in bringing about price reductions and improved service, the international airline industry has not been affected and is still being protected from competition. No country has the authority to liberalize the international airline industry. As a result, international airfares remain high despite much lower fuel prices in the last two years and service remains inadequate with crowded or fully booked planes on most routes.

A practical scheme to liberalize the international airline industry should be based on a clear understanding of the actual market situation. Table 2 shows the market situation between Hong Kong and sixteen other major countries. The figures show the share of Hong Kong's Cathay Pacific and the airlines of each paired country in third and fourth freedom traffic between April 1986 and March 1987. The country that has the largest volume of traffic with Hong Kong is Japan. In 1986/87, 1,648,831 passengers flew from a city in Japan to Hong Kong or from Hong Kong to a city in Japan through third and fourth freedom traffic. Note that a passenger who took off from a city in Japan, arrived in Hong Kong, and then went back to a city in Japan (it need not be the same city) is counted as two movements. In addition, 248,264 Japan/Hong Kong movements were recorded through fifth freedom traffic, i.e., these passengers travelled from a city in Japan to Hong Kong or vice versa on board a plane that belonged to an airline of a third country, for example, United or Northwest. In share terms, Japan Air Lines has a slight advantage (52.3%) over Cathay Pacific (47.1%). Japan Asia Airways accounts for a mere 0.6%. These figures confirm the belief that Japan Air Lines and Cathay Pacific exercise monopoly power over the market and share almost equally the traffic between themselves. Fifth freedom traffic has not reached threatening proportions. The bulk of the passengers on the Asian routes of United and Northwest (which accounted for most of the fifth freedom traffic) originated or terminated their journeys in the U.S., although some might stop over briefly in Tokyo. Therefore, the American airlines are hardly competing with Japan Air Lines and Cathay Pacific in these markets.

Taiwan has the second highest volume of traffic with Hong Kong. The total third and fourth freedom movements are about 1.2 million with China Airlines accounting for 55.7% of them. Fifth freedom traffic is however, relatively heavy with 426,694 movements recorded, the bulk of which is carried by Korean Air, Singapore Airlines and Thai Airways. These figures suggest that, while Taiwan and Hong Kong are joint monopolists, Taiwan might have been more generous than Japan in the granting of fifth freedom routes.

A similar situation occurs with Thailand, where Thai Airways has a 55.7% share over third/fourth freedom traffic. There is also a sizable proportion of fifth freedom traffic. Interestingly, more than half of the fifth freedom movements are accounted for by China Airlines, suggesting that Taiwan and Thailand might have been exchanging their fifth freedom rights with the (tacit) cooperation of Hong Kong.

While in the cases of Japan, Taiwan and Thailand, Cathay Pacific "loses" to foreign airlines in market share, in the case of the Philippines, Cathay Pacific and Philippine Airlines are even in market share. Moreover, there is no fifth freedom traffic.

The fact that Cathay Pacific "loses" market share to foreign airlines even in a monopoly situation is strongly illustrated in the case of Singapore. Out of a total volume of 635,990 movements, Cathay Pacific accounts for 34.7%, as opposed to 65.3% for Singapore Airlines. What is more astounding is that United Airlines manages to capture 103,965 movements out of 234,024 fifth freedom movements on its San Francisco-Hongkong-Singapore route. The reasons for Cathay Pacific's relatively poor performance in Singapore may be complicated and may lie in its flight pattern, take-off and landing times, marketing strategies, agency rebates, the support of package tours and ethnicity factor (while 80,023 Hong Kong residents travelled to Singapore in 1986, 172,904 Singaporeans, who might prefer Singapore

Airlines to Cathay Pacific, came to Hong Kong in the same year).[1]

In the case of the U.S., Northwest and United dominate third/fourth freedom traffic. Northwest had eleven weekly flights from the U.S. and United had twenty-four, while Cathay Pacific introduced its fourth in May and fifth in July, 1986. All fifth freedom traffic was carried by Singapore Airlines, which had seven weekly flights. We therefore observe that Singapore Airlines is actually stronger than Cathay Pacific in the Singapore-Hongkong-U.S. markets. All U.S.-bound traffic carried by Singapore Airlines stopped over in Hong Kong. It is not surprising that Singapore Airlines' repeated requests to the Hong Kong Government to be allowed more U.S.-bound flights were refused.

Fifth freedom traffic did not exist between Hong Kong and the U.K. or Australia in 1986. For both the U.K. and Australia, an even market share was maintained by each of them with Hong Kong.

Both South Korea and Malaysia maintained a slight advantage over Cathay Pacific with a 60-40 share of third/fourth freedom traffic. Fifth freedom traffic was relatively insignificant. In the case of South Korea, the fifth freedom traffic was carried by Thai Airways, while in the case of Malaysia, by China Airlines. A similar pattern but on a much smaller scale is seen in the case of Indonesia, whose flag carrier is Garuda. It accounts for 82,460 movements or 56.4% of third/fourth freedom traffic.

Canada is one country which has been losing market share to Hong Kong through the years. In 1986/87, Cathay Pacific overtook Canadian Airlines International by accounting for 57% of the traffic. One reason for this was that, while Cathay Pacific had been increasing the number of flights (five weekly flights by the end of 1986), Canadian Airlines had not (four weekly flights

---

[1] See *Hong Kong Tourist Association Annual Report 1985/86* and *Overseas Travel by Hong Kong Residents 1987.*

by the end of 1986). Another reason was that Cathay utilized Boeing 747 jets (capacity 412 passengers) while Canadian Airlines utilized DC10 jets (capacity 255 passengers). The remaining countries in Table 2 are all European countries. Traffic volume for each of these countries is relatively insignificant. Despite the sketchy nature of the figures, it seems that Lufthansa, Alitalia, Air France and KLM are not as competitive as Cathay Pacific. This supports the belief that, in general, the European airlines are not very competitive.[2] Although Cathay Pacific lost market share to Air France and KLM in 1986/87, it did not operate as many direct flights to Paris and Amsterdam as did Air France and KLM respectively. In 1986/87, Cathay only operated Hongkong-Paris-Rome and Hongkong-Frankfurt-Amsterdam flights. Therefore the capacity available for each city was rather limited.

The Scheme

A scheme is proposed that would use Hong Kong, a major hub in the global aviation network, as the starting point of a process to liberalize the international airline industry. Because of the decentralized nature of the industry and the time airlines require to take delivery of new planes, the process of liberalization would not be immediate. Although the process could be divided into three phases, Hong Kong would only need to take action in the first phase. Passengers in Hong Kong would quickly enjoy price reductions and the Hong Kong economy would receive a strong boost through its tourist industry as many more tourists would almost certainly visit Hong Kong as a result of the scheme.

The idea of the scheme, which is called a "Sequential Bilateral Liberalization" (SBL) scheme, is actually very simple. Hong Kong, after 1997 will be endowed with the authority to

---

2   See Pryke (1987) and Sawers (1987) for extensive discussion.

negotiate bilateral landing rights with other countries. This power is specifically mentioned in the Sino-British Joint Declaration and confirmed in the Draft of the Basic Law. In anticipation of the restoration of sovereignty to China, Hong Kong has already negotiated and signed a bilateral air services agreement with the Netherlands. In the past, the Government of the United Kingdom represented Hong Kong in the negotiations. The Hong Kong Government maintained its presence by sending only one or two officials to participate in the negotiations. For ease of discussion, the SBL scheme can be subdivided into three phases.

Phase One

In Phase One, the Hong Kong Government would attempt to open up completely routes to some major countries. Under bilateral open skies agreement, Hong Kong airlines would be allowed to make an unlimited number of flights to the other country, and in turn the other country's airlines would be allowed to have an unlimited number of flights into Hong Kong. In other words, this would be similar to a bilateral free trade agreement. Under the agreement, an airline could adjust the number of flights according to its own demand and cost conditions without regard for the repercussion that a matching change would have to be allowed the other country's airlines. If Cathay Pacific found that the Hongkong-Tokyo market was profitable, more flights could be supplied for that market. What had in the past been a joint monopoly market would become an open market for airlines in these two countries who would be competing against each other for more passengers by lowering prices and improving service. This would be the first step towards introducing competition into the industry.

Phase Two

Not all countries that are presently maintaining flights to Hong

Kong would be willing to go into a liberalization agreement with Hong Kong, so the impact of Phase One would be limited. The reason is that a foreign country might fear that Cathay Pacific or Dragonair might expand their volume at the expense of its own flag carrier. Some unprofitable airlines are already subsidized by governments, so any loss in traffic volume would put financial pressure on the government, which would therefore resist any liberalization initiative. Fortunately, even if there were restrictions on third and fourth freedom traffic between two countries, competition could still be introduced by expanding a combination of third and fourth freedom traffic involving a third country.[3] For example, say Canada was unwilling to open up the Vancouver-Hongkong market with Hong Kong, but the U.S. was willing to open up the Seattle-Hongkong market. The price for a Seattle-Hongkong trip would have to be much lower than that of a Vancouver-Hongkong trip because of more intense competition in the former. It is likely that a lot of Vancouver passengers would take advantage of this lower price by making a short trip from Vancouver to Seattle and then onward to Hong Kong instead of flying directly from Vancouver. If the Vancouver-Seattle flow of passengers were sizable, the U.S. airlines would adjust their flight times to make the transfer a convenient one. This would impose competitive pressure on Canadian Airlines. To regain its volume, it would really have only two options. The first would be to ask the Canadian and Hong Kong governments to allow it to make more flights to Hong Kong or reduce the price so as to match the Vancouver-Seattle-Hongkong price. The second would be to maintain the current number of flights and the current price but improve the quality of service. Both options would benefit the passengers, perhaps a combination of both options may be the most likely outcome because there is a limit beyond which service cannot be improved without making cheaper price a more cost-effective

---

[3] This is informally called sixth freedom as discussed in Chapter 3.

alternative. The conclusion is that, even if there were countries that refused to open up routes with Hong Kong initially, by entering into liberalization agreements with neighbour countries, the SBL scheme would still encourage liberalization between these countries and Hong Kong. By liberalizing with major countries in Phase One so as to cover a large geographical area, the success of Phase Two could be ensured. The result is that Hong Kong travellers would enjoy cheaper airfares to even more destinations.

Phase Three

Suppose the SBL scheme had reached the stage where a significant number of countries have entered into liberalization agreements with Hong Kong. The situation, unlike the U.S. domestic airline industry, would still be far from a totally liberalized one in which any airline could supply any number of flights to serve a route of its choice and at a self-determined price. The Hong Kong Government has the right to permit planes to land in Hong Kong, but not in any other city. How could it bring about liberalization between say, Taiwan and Singapore? Suppose Hong Kong had liberalization agreements with Singapore, and Hong Kong's airlines had liberalization agreements with China Airlines. It would be in the interests of Singapore and Taiwan to have a liberalization agreement with each other.[4]

The reason is easy to see. Because of the bilateral agreements with Hong Kong, there would be many flights serving the Taiwan-Hongkong and Singapore-Hongkong routes. Prices for these flights would be cheap. Passengers who wanted to travel Taiwan-Singapore or vice versa would find it attractive

---

[4] For diplomatic reasons, there is no bilateral air services agreement between the U.K. and Taiwan that would apply to Hong Kong. At present Cathay Pacific has commercial agreements with China Airlines.

to choose Hong Kong as a stopover point. The Taiwan-Singapore direct flights would suffer as a result. To stay competitive, these direct flights would have to be cheaper. Alternatively, they might try to offer better service to attract passengers in the short-term. But as shown earlier, cheaper prices seem to be the only viable solution in the long-term. However, cheaper prices would have to be accompanied by an increase in traffic volume in order to cover overhead costs. Therefore, Taiwan and Singapore would negotiate to increase the number of direct flights. As passenger demand changed from year to year, frequent negotiations between them would have to take place. The governments would soon realize that relaxing all restrictions and leaving the airlines to compete against each other for the market share in the Taiwan-Singapore markets would be a much more economical method of settlement. Ultimately, these governments would be obliged to have a liberalization agreement between them. In addition, China Airlines could then freely enter Hongkong-Singapore markets and Singapore Airlines could freely enter Hongkong-Taiwan markets. Thus, competition in these markets would become even more intense and service would improve further.

In Phase Three of the scheme, Hong Kong would play an intermediary role in inducing global liberalization. Having liberalized with two other countries individually and bilaterally, the two countries would be encouraged in time to liberalize between themselves. It is argued that this conclusion holds for most cases, but may be seen by some as an over-generalization. The previous Taiwan-Singapore example has been chosen with some care. Hong Kong is so geographically situated that it presents itself as a convenient stopover point between Singapore and Taiwan. Flying direct between Singapore and Taiwan does not save a lot of distance. To the passenger, an indirect flight through Hong Kong would not be particularly bothersome. But if we replace Taiwan in the example with Australia, then, as Hong Kong is not a convenient stopover point for Australia-Singapore flights, the previous conclusion will not hold. Even with separate liberalization agreements between Hong Kong and Australia, and Hong Kong and Singapore (achieved in Phase One and Phase Two), Australia and Singapore might have no incentive to liberalize between themselves. This criticism no doubt holds equally well with any two countries which are close to each other but both far from Hong Kong. Examples are the U.S. and Canada, Australia and New Zealand, Indonesia and the Philippines, and indeed any two European countries.

One should not overlook an important point. In granting landing rights freely under the SBL scheme, planes from all surrounding cities would converge on Hong Kong. The increased traffic would benefit Hong Kong, providing more business for hotels, restaurants and retail firms. Other cities would learn from the success of liberalization in Hong Kong and contemplate liberalization of flights that originate and terminate in their cities. They would realize that under liberalization, the gainers are firstly, the passengers as they enjoy lower airfares and better services; secondly, tourist-related and passenger-related businesses such as hotels, restaurants, etc.; and thirdly, the government because of increased airport and profit taxes. The losers would be much fewer. Initially, the country's own airlines would be exposed to competitive pressure. If the airline was strong, liberalization would be welcomed. It would create opportunities for growth and expansion. It is only in the case of a weak airline that resistance to liberalization would be likely. Management would fear that competition might aggravate its financial problems and workers would fear that their remuneration package would suffer and the room for bargaining for raises be much reduced. In this situation, a government would weigh the political costs against the benefits of liberalization.

If a country has a strong airline such as Singapore, Taiwan, Thailand, South Korea, Japan, the U.K. and the U.S., a liberalization initiative would be much welcomed. If each of these countries adopted the SBL scheme and liberalized not only with Hong Kong but with other countries as well, a large step would have been taken towards global liberalization. The large hubs in Asia would be Hong Kong, Singapore, Tokyo, Bangkok; and the smaller ones, Taipei and Seoul. The large hubs in North America would be Los Angeles, San Francisco, Chicago and New York; and a smaller one, Seattle. The global network over North America and Asia would then be largely liberalized.

The last completing step towards global liberalization would probably involve the European countries. European airlines are not competitive in general and European countries are very defensive in the granting of air routes.[5] Airlines of the U.S. have encountered much frustration in their attempts to expand their network in Europe. The result is that European airfares are generally higher than American airfares. It might seem that European countries would be reluctant to liberalize the industry. Recent developments give reason for some optimism.

Firstly, the average growth rate of European countries has been increasing in recent years. This is having the desirable effect of causing an increase in air traffic, thus increasing the need for flexible route patterns and increased flights. Moreover, larger sales volumes should limit the losses of inefficient airlines following liberalization, hence reducing their resistance.

Secondly, privatization and deregulation are spreading in the U.K. The present government believes in the free play of market forces. The previous beliefs in regulation and protection are out of fashion. Furthermore, the two airports at London, Heathrow and Gatwick, make London the largest hub in Europe. The traffic that London itself generates plus the transfer and transit passengers (owing to its central location) would yield huge gains to the U.K. after liberalization.

Thirdly, European countries are becoming increasingly aware of the benefits of free trade among themselves. If free trade is possible, free air routes should also be possible. While it is true that large and small airlines now coexist and liberalization

---

5 See Sawers (1987).

poses the danger of driving out small firms, the possibility of sharing maintenance facilities and reservation systems makes it likely that small airlines in Europe could still survive under liberalization. Moreover, European airlines could move up market to serve consumers who were not concerned about price. Therefore, there is much hope that European countries would liberalize among themselves, while the U.K. would go further in liberalizing with other world countries and capture a large share of the traffic that originates from and terminates in Europe. Global liberalization is not unrealistic.

Analyzing Business Performance by Load Factors

In order to identify the countries that Hong Kong might approach for bilateral liberalization with likely success in Phase One of the scheme, we need to know the performance of different airlines that are currently serving Hong Kong. Available data are sketchy because airlines are unwilling to disclose their business figures to their rivals.

An index of airline performance is the load factor, which is defined as the number of passengers flown as a percentage of available capacity between two points. A low load factor indicates an airline that is not preferred by passengers for reasons such as poor service, lack of goodwill or inadequate marketing strategies (including uncompetitive rebate packages for the agents). Such an airline would probably resist liberalization for fear of business being lost to the current monopolistic partner or to newcomers. On the other hand, a very high load factor does not necessarily indicate a very competitive airline that is keen to liberalize. Such an airline is failing to maximize sales (hence profit) by restricting the number of flights. There may be two reasons for this. The first reason may be that the monopolistic partner country restricts the number of flights and so the airline cannot expand. The second reason may be that the airline is poorly managed and fails to supply flights to meet passenger demand, or that the airline is simply not profit-maximizing because of lack of incentives and bureaucracy.

For bilateral liberalization to work in the circumstance when a Hong Kong airline is inefficient in a particular market it would be necessary to convince the government that the public interest as a whole should have priority over the profit of a Hong Kong airline. If the stumbling block is due to the intransigence of the other government and diplomatic negotiations failed, we could continue with our liberalization effort with other countries and allow market developments to gradually change their views about opening up their markets. Recall that market pressure would be generated by liberalizing with countries that were close to the country that was unwilling to liberalize, hence diverting traffic through those countries (as in the Vancouver-Seattle-Hongkong case discussed above in connection with Phase Two of the scheme).

Table 3 shows the average load factor of each of the thirty airlines that served scheduled passenger flights to Hong Kong in 1986/87. The average load factor for arrivals of an airline (similarly for departures) in 1986/87 is calculated by dividing the total number of passengers that were flown to Hong Kong by that airline in 1986/87 by the total number of seats that were available. The load factor of each market (a city pair), although ideal for facilitating comparison between airlines in the same market, is a badly defined concept in practice. Airlines typically run many indirect flights. For example, Cathay Pacific has a San Francisco-Vancouver-Hongkong flight. One cannot calculate a load factor for the Vancouver-Hongkong market or the San Francisco-Hongkong market separately because the capacity available for each is not identifiable. Table 4 shows the average load factor calculations but includes both transit and transfer passengers, while Table 3 excludes transit passengers.

To facilitate discussion a rule of thumb can be adopted. If the average load factor of an airline is less than 0.6 (a number which is much lower than the industry average) for both arrivals and departures (including transit passengers), it is assumed that

Table 3
Load Factors for Flights Serving Hong Kong
without Transit Passengers

Airline	one way scheduled passenger flights	one way seat capacity in 1986	market volume (1986/87)		average load factor	
			Arrival	Departure	Arrival	Departure
Air India	312	117,624	35,822	32,748	0.3045	0.2784
Air France	156	46,124	34,749	34,113	0.7534	0.7396
Air Lanka	104	28,080	22,775	22,613	0.8111	0.8053
Air Nauru	52	4,836	602	842	0.1245	0.1741
Alitalia	260	75,400	32,672	35,743	0.4333	0.4740
British Airways	416	155,168	106,821	105,721	0.6884	0.6813
British Caledonian	364	107,276	68,633	68,840	0.6398	0.6417
Canadian Pacific	208	53,040	34,593	43,234	0.6522	0.8151
Cathay Pacific	6,916	2,451,904	1,846,272	1,849,275	0.7530	0.7542
China Airlines	3,276	784,056	475,514	488,363	0.6065	0.6229
CAAC	2,860	433,212	437,757	424,574	1.0105	0.9801
Dragonair	208	26,208	27,188	31,899	1.0374	1.2171
Garuda	468	126,256	69,373	80,359	0.5495	0.6365
Gulf Air	104	24,960	8,469	8,224	0.3393	0.3295
Japan Air L.	2,080	620,048	474,273	485,848	0.7649	0.7836
Japan Asia A.	364	99,372	51,838	54,987	0.5217	0.5533
KLM	104	29,952	11,382	11,427	0.3800	0.3815
Korean A.L.	520	162,344	134,417	134,695	0.8280	0.8297
Lufthansa	260	85,020	40,458	49,928	0.4759	0.5873
Malaysian A.S.	728	204,828	116,029	115,151	0.5665	0.5622
Northwest	572	228,800	122,266	156,294	0.5344	0.6831
Philippine A.	780	193,336	177,231	171,989	0.9167	0.8896
Qantas	416	166,712	103,618	120,405	0.6215	0.7222
Royal Brunei	104	15,392	8,365	8,266	0.5435	0.5370
Royal Nepal	208	21,424	17,598	17,860	0.8214	0.8336
Singapore A.	1,248	509,184	323,783	349,146	0.6359	0.6857
South African A.	52	15,704	12,583	11,388	0.8013	0.7252
Swissair	416	104,416	43,924	44,897	0.4207	0.4300
Thai Airways I.	2,548	629,356	365,979	342,143	0.5815	0.5436
United Airlines	1,612	426,764	253,189	279,545	0.5933	0.6550
All Scheduled Operators	27,716	7,946,796	5,458,173	5,580,517	0.6868	0.7022
Flying Tiger Line & Nippon Cargo			3,488	421		
			5,458,521	5,580,938		

Notes: 1. Market volume refers to year April 1986 - March 1987. Transfer passengers are included but transit passengers are excluded.

2. Seat capacity does not include capacity from charter flights. Market volume includes passengers from charter flights. Hence average load factors can be larger than 1, particularly for airlines that ran a lot of charter flights during April 1986 - March 1987.

Source: Report on Civil Aviation Hong Kong 1986-1987
Hong Kong Tourist Association Annual Report 1985/86

Table 4
Load Factors for Flights Serving Hong Kong with Transit Passengers

Airline	one way seat capacity in 1986	market volume (1986/87) Arrival	Departure	average load factor Arrival	Departure
Air India	117,624	83,364	80,290	0.7087	0.6826
Air France	46,124	34,749	34,113	0.7534	0.7396
Air Lanka	28,080	27,640	27,478	0.9843	0.9786
Air Nauru	4,836	602	842	0.1245	0.1741
Alitalia	75,400	70,565	73,636	0.9359	0.9766
British Airways	155,168	119,143	117,751	0.7678	0.7589
British Caledonian	107,276	68,633	68,840	0.6398	0.6417
Canadian Pacific	53,040	34,593	43,234	0.6522	0.8151
Cathay Pacific	2,451,904	1,846,272	1,849,275	0.7530	0.7542
China Airlines	784,056	601,215	613,926	0.7668	0.7830
CAAC	433,212	437,757	424,574	1.0105	0.9801
Dragonair	26,208	27,188	31,899	1.0374	1.2171
Garuda	126,256	69,373	80,359	0.5495	0.6365
Gulf Air	24,960	8,469	8,224	0.3393	0.3295
Japan Air L.	620,048	508,286	519,861	0.8198	0.8384
Japan A.A.	99,372	51,838	54,987	0.5217	0.5533
KLM	29,952	11,382	11,427	0.3800	0.3815
Korean A.L.	162,344	134,420	134,698	0.8280	0.8297
Lufthansa	85,020	40,458	49,928	0.4759	0.5873
Malaysia A.S.	204,828	171,601	170,723	0.8378	0.8335
Northwest	228,800	122,513	156,541	0.5355	0.6842
Philippine A.	193,336	177,353	172,111	0.9173	0.8902
Qantas	166,712	104,120	121,028	0.6246	0.7260
Royal Brunei	15,392	8,365	8,266	0.5435	0.5370
Royal Nepal	21,424	17,598	17,860	0.8214	0.8336
Singapore A.	509,184	394,216	419,434	0.7742	0.8237
South Africa A.	15,704	12,583	11,388	0.8013	0.7252
Swissair	104,416	60,918	61,891	0.5834	0.5927
Thai Airways I.	629,356	441,348	417,476	0.7013	0.6633
United Airlines	426,764	272,818	299,098	0.6393	0.7009
All Scheduled Operators	7,946,796	5,959,380	6,081,158	0.7499	0.7653
Flying Tiger Line & Nippon Cargo		368	443		
		5,959,748	6,081,601		

Notes:
1. Market volume refers to year April 1986 - March 1987. Transfer passengers are included.
2. Seat capacity does not include capacity from charter flights. Market volume includes passengers from charter flights. Hence average load factors can be larger than 1, particularly for airlines that ran a lot of charter flights during April 1986 - March 1987.

Source: Report on Civil Aviation Hong Kong 1986 -1987
Hong Kong Tourist Association Annual Report 1985/86

these routes are not lucrative enough to warrant large expansions. Those countries whose airlines are operating these routes might not be enthusiastic about liberalizing with Hong Kong.[6] There are seven such airlines: Air Nauru, Gulf Air, Japan Asia Airways, KLM, Lufthansa, Royal Brunei and Swissair.

Also, as argued previously, airlines that "enjoy" a particularly high load factor may resist liberalization under some circumstances. Since little is publicly known about the exact reasons for the high load factors of these airlines, it is best to omit them from the discussion. For simplicity, take this to mean any airline with a load factor of more than 0.8 for both arrivals and departures. This includes Air Lanka, Korean Air, Philippine Airlines and Royal Nepal.

Finally, one observes that a number of airlines suffer from low passenger volume on their Hong Kong flights. There is not much opportunity for them to expand their Hong Kong routes. Liberalization with Hong Kong would probably not bring them much benefit. The countries of these airlines should not be among the first that Hong Kong should approach for liberalization. Using a one-way traffic volume of a hundred thousand passengers a year as a cut off point, those airlines which are serving "thin" markets, but are otherwise enjoying moderately high load factors can be eliminated. These include: Air India, Air France, Alitalia, Canadian Airlines, Garuda and South African Airways.

After eliminating those airlines with either very low or very high load factors and those serving "thin" markets, we are left with eight countries. The airlines of these eight countries tend to be competitive, aggressive, and are sharing heavy traffic markets with the two Hong Kong airlines, Cathay Pacific and Dragonair. These eight countries are: Australia, Malaysia, Japan, the U.S., the U.K., Singapore, Thailand and Taiwan. Together, these

---

[6] Air traffic volume fluctuates seasonally. An average load factor of 0.6 over the year in both arrivals and departures is thus pretty low.

countries cover all the essential hubs in the global air traffic network. If Hong Kong succeeds in liberalizing with all or most of these eight countries in Phase One, then Phase Two (liberalization with countries that are in the neighbourhood of the eight) and even Phase Three (inducing liberalization among other countries) would probably materialize in time.

The Countries for Phase One Deliberalization

In this section, we combine the information on the market share, average load factor and route structure of each airline to outline the likely benefits and costs of bilateral liberalization with each of the eight suggested countries.[7] Of course, if other countries should wish to liberalize with Hong Kong, the Hong Kong Government should also welcome their initiative.

(1) The United States of America

The U.S. is a country that advocates free trade and deregulation except for those sectors where there are strong organised vested interests. The domestic airline deregulation in 1978 has, by and large, achieved desirable results such as lower airfares, increased services to most cities, more price-quality variation and greatly expanded traffic volume. Americans should welcome liberalization opportunities in the international industry as well. Furthermore, the U.S. is the single largest aircraft manufacturing country in the free world. The huge demand for additional aircraft as a result of global liberalization would greatly benefit the aircraft industry and the balance of payments.

If the Hong Kong Government initiated bilateral liberalization negotiations with the U.S. Government, the Americans may find the proposal attractive. At present the Hongkong-U.S. markets are dominated by United and

---

[7] Because of space limitations, the following discussion is much shortened.

Northwest. The principle of free flights conforms to stated free market philosophy. In addition, the Pacific division has high growth potential. The most lucrative routes are between the west coast of the U.S. and Japan. However, the attempt to expand into the Japanese markets has been repeatedly frustrated due to Japanese protectionism. Liberalization with Hong Kong would create the prospect of inducing Japan to open up its markets. Boeing 747 jets are capable of direct flights from Hong Kong to any city on the west coast without making stopovers in between. In other words, passengers going to a city in Japan or the rest of Asia might transfer or transit in Hong Kong instead of in a city in Japan. Any additional time cost would in part be compensated for by cheaper airfares.

The bulk of U.S.-Hongkong traffic is carried by the two American airlines United and Northwest. Cathay Pacific, even under liberalization could not pose an immediate threat. Firstly, the size of its fleet would restrict quick expansion on American routes. Secondly, Cathay lacks convenient linkages with U.S. domestic flights. Thirdly, a passenger's choice of airline depends on an ethnicity factor, i.e. Americans favour American airlines. Although about a hundred thousand Hong Kong residents travel to the U.S. every year, almost seven times that number of U.S. residents travel to Hong Kong every year.[8] The ethnicity factor guarantees the American airlines a large market share, probably even after liberalization.

(2) Japan

The second country that the Government might attempt to liberalize bilaterally with would be Japan. Japan is by tradition very protectionist oriented. Its government would have to be convinced that Japan stood to gain a lot from liberalization.

It was observed previously that Japan is the largest air

---

[8] See the Hong Kong Tourist Association publications.

market for Hong Kong. For the following reasons Japan could gain substantially from liberalization. Firstly, the Japan-Hongkong market is likely to grow quickly as Japanese tourists and businessmen travel more frequently as a result of income growth and increased overseas investment. Liberalization would bring flexibility, especially in the interconnections between domestic and international flights. Cathay Pacific is at a disadvantage in this respect. Secondly, under liberalization, Japanese airlines could capture the markets between Hong Kong and other cities. Thirdly, the Japanese government increasingly favours open competition between Japan Air Lines, Air Nippon Airways and Japan Asia Airways. Liberalization would enhance such competition. Fourthly, if Hong Kong was successful in liberalizing with the U.S., Japanese airlines and Japanese airports would lose business and there would be pressure for Japan to liberalize.

Liberalization might well be beneficial to both sides. Cathay would not likely lose under liberalization. While the ethnicity factor would probably prevent Cathay Pacific from gaining in the Hongkong-Japan markets, much could be gained from flights beyond Japan. If the U.S. had already liberalized, Cathay Pacific could capture much traffic from Japan-U.S. (especially west coast) markets.

(3) Taiwan

Like Japan, Taiwan generates a lot of traffic. Given its economic prosperity and the increasing tendency for capital to find outlets overseas, traffic volume would grow. Liberalization would be desirable to both Taiwan and Hong Kong.

There are also other reasons for liberalization. Taiwan, with Kaoshiung and Taipei being its international airports, has no direct flight services to China, any country in Europe, Canada or Australia, despite the recent surge in demand in these markets. Cathay Pacific, by contrast, serves direct flights to all these areas. Under liberalization, China Airlines could receive a strong boost in sales by funneling all the Taiwanese outgoing traffic to Hong Kong, which would become a gateway to the world via Cathay Pacific flights; and it could even capture traffic beyond Hong Kong.

But Cathay Pacific would have more to gain. Cathay Pacific might use Taipei as a stopping point for its U.S. flights and thus capture some Taiwan-U.S. traffic. If the U.S. and Japan were already liberalized, Hongkong-U.S. markets would be very competitive because at least seven airlines from the U.S., Japan, Taiwan and Hong Kong could compete against each other and benefit the consumers by offering very low airfares.

(4) Thailand

Bangkok, where the major international airport of Thailand is situated, is a large hub in Asia. It has direct flight services to all the major cities in the world. In addition, the government is sensitive to the needs of traffic growth and a new terminal has just come into operation.

Thai Airways International, the flag carrier of Thailand, should favour liberalization with Hong Kong. Thai Airways has an efficient domestic network as well as a local network with Singapore, Malaysia and Indonesia. Under liberalization, Thai Airways could augment the feeder traffic from within Thailand and from nearby countries to Hong Kong and, at the same time capture the markets for flights beyond Hong Kong. For example, Hongkong-U.S. and Hongkong-Canada flights, both of which command sizable volume, could be introduced. Thai Airways could also introduce indirect flights from Bangkok to North America making one stopover in Hong Kong.

The flight opportunities beyond Hong Kong that Thai Airways might gain could affect Cathay Pacific negatively. Passengers who depart from Hong Kong for North America would have more airlines to choose from. Also, passengers who originate in Thailand would probably choose Thai Airways because it could offer a lower price for the entire trip and more convenience in transiting. This loss in traffic, however, must be balanced against some likely gain in traffic. For example, passengers originating from S. Korea, the U.S., Tokyo and China, and bound for Thailand, would find it convenient to stopover in Hong Kong and take advantage of the many Cathay Pacific flights to Thailand.

(5) *Singapore*

Singapore is a metropolitan city, it generates a lot of traffic, and is a major hub in Asia serving direct flights to all major world cities. Singapore is similar to Thailand for the purposes of analysis, except that Singapore has no need for a domestic airline network. The same analysis that applies to Thailand applies equally well to Singapore.

The Hong Kong Government recently refused Singapore's request for more flights beyond Hong Kong. Singapore Airlines had wanted to increase the frequencies of its Singapore-Hongkong-Honolulu and Singapore-Hongkong-San Francisco flights. Their frustration with the Hong Kong government is evidence that it is eager to expand its service and would certainly welcome liberalization with Hong Kong.

As in the case with Thai Airways, Singapore Airlines would have much to gain by liberalization, but Cathay Pacific might suffer a slight loss. It was indicated earlier that in terms of market share Singapore Airlines has an advantage over Cathay Pacific in the Hongkong-Singapore and Hongkong-U.S. markets. Furthermore, Cathay Pacific would gain little from beyond-Singapore flight opportunities. Singapore cannot be used as a gateway to any major city, except for those in Australia and New Zealand, to which Cathay Pacific is already serving direct flights.

If the Hong Kong Government successfully liberalized with Japan, Taiwan, Thailand and Singapore, the four countries would quickly liberalize among themselves. Since all of them are relatively close to each other, failure to liberalize would result in loss of business to the Hong Kong airport and airlines. If they liberalized, then the regional network of Asia would be essentially liberalized. The gains to the consumers would be enormous. Airfares would be lower, service better at current prices and flights more frequent.

(6) The United Kingdom

London, with Heathrow and Gatwick as its international airports, is the largest hub in Europe. At present, it is the communications centre of Europe. All the large cities in Europe are linked by daily direct flights to London.

The London-Hongkong traffic volume is shared by three airlines: British Airways, British Caledonian Airways and Cathay Pacific. There is no fifth freedom traffic. If the Asian countries continue to grow at their historical rates, Asia-Europe traffic volume will expand quickly. With Hong Kong being a major hub in Asia and London a major hub in Europe, Asia-Europe traffic can be efficiently built up along the London-Hongkong route. Passengers who originate from Asia can converge on Hong Kong via feeder routes which would be very convenient if the Asian countries liberalized with Hong Kong. Similarly, passengers originating from European countries can converge on London via the existing feeder routes. If the U.K. liberalized with Hong Kong, then flights along the London-Hongkong route would be able to expand sufficiently to accommodate the increase in demand. The essential condition for this scenario to happen is that regional liberalization has gone far enough so that the transfer from feeder routes to the long-haul London-Hongkong route was convenient enough to attract consumers away from taking a direct flight. Thirty-three flights a week one-way between London and Hong Kong might be sufficient to attract Asian passengers to stop over in Hong Kong and European passengers to stop over in London. This would mean adding only one more daily flight to the current schedule of twenty-six flights a week. With liberalization, the additional flights could be accommodated by the three airlines.

(7) Australia

The present Australian Government has indicated that it intends to allow more competition between the two Australian airlines, Qantas and Ansett. Liberalization would provide the opportunity to increase the number of flights out of Australia necessary for effective competition.

The isolated location of Australia makes the consequences of liberalization easier to foresee. Also because of its isolation, few direct flights are serving Australia internationally. Both Australian airlines would gain if more Australian flights could stop over in Hong Kong. They could run many flights beyond Hong Kong to the U.S., Europe, Japan and South Korea. Because of the large number of flights that originate from Hong Kong, passengers could obtain quick transfers to other cities as well. Fewer stop-overs would be made in other Asian hubs. These hubs would lose to Hong Kong, and the Hong Kong airport and the Hong Kong tourist industry would get more business. On the other hand, Cathay Pacific might lose slightly as its Australian routes came under increased competition and it could not use Australia as a stopover point for flights beyond. The extent of business loss would depend on how well Cathay Pacific could meet the market test under competition. In any case, the consumers would gain from increased competition.

(8) Malaysia

The fact that the Malaysian economy is strongly linked to the Singaporean economy means that strong air linkages must exist between Malaysia and Singapore. This is in fact the case. If Hong Kong liberalized with Singapore, then Malaysia would have to liberalize with Hong Kong. Malaysians who head for Hong Kong and beyond would otherwise simply transfer or transit in Singapore, which under liberalization would serve frequent flights to Hong Kong.

Some Queries

The reader might have some queries concerning the liberalization scheme. The following attempts to provide answers to these queries.

(1) Would it be premature to suppose that countries of the world would liberalize air markets with Hong Kong or with other countries?

Liberalization benefits consumers and if governments act in their interest, then they should consider liberalization. Of course, it is conceivable that in some circumstances the interests of the airline and the consumers are not wholly aligned, a government might choose to put the interest of the airline company before the consumers, it would then refuse to liberalize. The difficulty with negotiating and concluding multilateral liberalization agreements is that any single country can veto it. The attraction of bilateral agreements is that it takes at a minimum only one foreign country to make it start working. So long as Hong Kong liberalizes, consumers in Hong Kong and elsewhere and related businesses would benefit from the increased traffic. In time, the success of Hong Kong might convince other countries of the benefits of liberalization.

(2) If after liberalization a few giant airlines should emerge through mergers and acquisitions, would it not renew the threat of collusion against the consumer?

The international airline industry is more complex than the U.S. domestic airline industry in some respects. In the international airline industry, perceived national prestige considerations plays a role in determining public policy. Governments might be reluctant to allow airline mergers, let alone acquisitions. Even if it were possible and giant airlines did emerge after liberalization, it does not follow that they would necessarily and successfully collude against consumer interests by charging airfares above competitive rates. Firstly, the anti-trust laws in some countries deter overt collusion. Secondly, under collusion an airline would always have the incentive to serve more flights and charge slightly lower airfares in order to capture more profits. The cartel would not be robust. Thirdly, even if the cartel was robust, other airlines could always enter the lucrative markets and undercut airfares. The capital outlay might be a deterrent for the smaller airlines to enter the long-haul flight markets. Nevertheless, the ready market for used planes and loan-financing should help overcome the capital barrier. In other words, giant airlines cannot charge above competitive rates.

(3) Consumers in some sparsely populated areas of the U.S. were worse off after the deregulation of the U.S. domestic industry. Would the same happen after liberalization of the international industry?

Before the U.S. deregulation, consumers in some areas were able to travel on subsidized direct flights which, after deregulation, were either stopped or reduced in frequency. The removal of subsidies meant that airfares could be higher after deregulation. The case with the international industry is different. Firstly, there is no evidence in support of the claim that some airlines in the industry are being subsidized in order to offer low airfares. On the contrary, the airlines which are most competitive are often the most profitable. Therefore, with increased competition after liberalization, airfares could only become lower. Secondly, the conjecture that some airlines might have been cross-subsidizing between routes does not hold logically. In an international context, why should an airline favour the travellers on some particular routes? It would imply the airline was not profit-maximizing. Even if this were the case for some particular reason, why should the consumers on certain routes subsidize those on the favoured routes? In Hong Kong, both Cathay Pacific and Dragonair are private airlines. Since there is no evidence suggesting cross-subsidization between routes, it is most unlikely that the airfares for any flight that originate or terminate in Hong Kong would go up after liberalization.

Conclusion

As a major hub in Asia, Hong Kong can play an important role in bringing about the liberalization of the international airline industry. A Sequential Bilateral Liberalization scheme is proposed, which involves negotiating and concluding bilateral liberalization agreements with interested countries. The pressure to liberalize would gather strength in the process as more and more countries entered into this kind of agreement. Eight countries which might respond positively to liberalization initiatives are identified, namely, the U.S., Japan, Taiwan, Thailand, Singapore, the U.K., Australian and Malaysia. They all maintain sizable traffic volume with Hong Kong and have efficient and aggressive airlines that are interested in pursuing opportunities for expansion. Hong Kong would benefit from liberalization through cheaper airfares, improved air services and increased economic activity in tourist-related businesses. The reputation of Hong Kong as a free trade and financial centre would be enhanced. As soon as some countries liberalize with Hong Kong, other countries may—for fear of loss of airline profits, airport and tourist business—begin to have an incentive to liberalize with Hong Kong. Over time, more countries would find it in their interest to liberalize among themselves. This would open the way to global liberalization of the airline industry in time.

The exact gains and losses to every interested party will be difficult to determine precisely owing to the complex nature of the industry. The U.S. experience with airline deregulation demonstrates clearly certain benefits to the consumer. Typically, more competition would exist among airlines leading to lower airfares, more price-quality choice, more frequent flights, increased traffic volume and greater responsiveness of airlines to consumer demands.

4   Congestion at Kai Tak Airport

Introduction

Liberalization would place heavy demand on airport facilities. It is therefore important that airport facilities are utilized efficiently. Few would dispute the claim that Hong Kong's Kai Tak Airport is one of the busiest in the world. Between April 1986 and March 1987, it saw 32,027 landings and 32,028 take-offs of scheduled flights. In the same year, some 5.5 million passengers passed through the airport in either direction. In growth terms, the figures are equally astounding. In the twenty years since 1967, passenger volume has grown almost nine times, equivalent to an annual rate of 11.6%. This fast growth reflects on one hand the growth of Hong Kong's economy and its importance as a financial and tourist centre and on the other hand the growth of the airline industry globally.

The fast growth of air traffic has created several problems, the most notable one being congestion at the airport terminal. Although the government has expanded the capacity of the terminal several times, capacity has not expanded quickly enough to accommodate the surge in demand. Considering the anticipated growth in traffic volume in the coming years, the slowness in response of the government and the lead time necessary for any construction for capacity expansion, the congestion problem is going to persist and may even worsen in the next decade. This would become even more so if the government liberalized the airline industry. The result will clearly be a badly congested airport where passengers, traffic controllers, immigration officers, customs officers, airline personnel, supporting staff, policemen, taxi and coach drivers all complain about inadequate facilities.

This will not only restrict the growth of air traffic and the advantages of liberalization, but also affect the reputation of Hong Kong as a convenient financial and tourist centre. A scheme to auction landing time slots is proposed here to alleviate the congestion problem.

Landing times may be auctioned to all airlines that want to land their planes in Hong Kong, including Cathay Pacific and Dragonair. The aim here is to devise a scheme that efficiently manages landings and take-offs. It is based on the principle that if a resource is scarce, it should be allocated to the producer who values it most. This principle applies to all airports that face congestion problems. The reader may believe that what Hong Kong needs is a new and larger airport. Clearly in the long run, no matter how efficiently the airport is managed, its physical capacity ultimately would become a binding constraint as traffic grows continuously. However, in the short-term, an auctioning scheme is clearly required to accommodate traffic growth while a new airport is being constructed. Furthermore, to avoid crowding in the airport terminal during peak hours and to maximize utilization of it, an auctioning scheme is equally desirable for the new airport.

Present Situation

According to Civil Aviation Department statistics, in the year from April 1986 to March 1987, there were 29,659 landings of passenger planes (27,404 of which were by scheduled flights, the rest mainly by charter flights) and 29,718 take-offs of passenger planes (27,418 of which were by scheduled flights, the rest mainly by charter flights). In addition, there were 2,294 cargo flight landings and 2,797 take-offs.[1] Since passenger flights account for the vast majority of air traffic, they will be the focus of the present discussion. In the year from April 1986 to March 1987,

---

[1] Figures taken from *Report on Civil Aviation Hong Kong 1986-1987.*

5,472,021 passengers arrived at the airport and 5,594,786 passengers departed. In addition, there were 502,376 transit passengers who merely stayed at the airport for a few hours before continuing with their journeys.[2] These annual figures translate into daily averages of eighty-one landings and eighty-one take-offs, 14,985 arriving passengers, 15,322 departing passengers and 1,376 transit passengers. In terms of growth, the number of landings and take-offs has grown by 2.1 times in the two decades since 1967 but the number of passengers (either arriving or departing) has grown by nine times in the same period, the difference being attributable to the use of more and more jumbo jets, which can carry in excess of four hundred passengers when fully occupied.

Kai Tak Airport has gone through several expansions in the last two decades, however, the surge in traffic volume has rendered these expansions inadequate. In 1987, the one-way capacity at the airport was 3,400 passengers per hour. The passenger flow in 1986/87 was of the magnitude that the thirtieth busiest hour in terms of arrivals recorded 3,334, and in terms of departures recorded 3,306. Both figures are close to design capacity. More flights were added in 1988. In the week starting April 11, 1988 for example, the average number of landings and take-offs was eighty-three each, as opposed to eighty-one each in 1986/87. One can safely predict that the flow in the thirty busiest hours in 1987/88 will far exceed the design capacity of 3,400 passengers per hour.

An interesting hypothetical question is, if the physical capacity of the terminal is kept fixed, what is the limit on the number of passengers it can handle? Suppose all airport personnel such as customs and immigration officers, security staff and airline

---

2 Scheduled airlines accounted for 5,458,521 arrivals, 5,580,938 departures and 501,227 transits. See Tables 3 and 4 for breakdown by airlines. Non-scheduled airlines accounted for 13,500 arrivals, 13,848 departures and 1,149 transits.

supporting personnel can be freely deployed so that no bottlenecks will form. Based on the fifteen daily opening hours from 8:00 to 23:00, the theoretical limit is 18.6 million passengers one-way in a year. Set against this limit, in 1986/87, the terminal was only about 30% utilized.

One may object to the above calculation by pointing out that it is likely that bottlenecks would be caused by such factors as the speed at which arriving passengers can be driven away from the airport by taxis, coaches, etc. While this might be true, it is also true that, at the moment, a lot of congestion is caused by an inefficient crowding of planes which land and depart within narrow time ranges. By regulating the number of planes that can land or take off in a given hour, a lot of congestion can be avoided.

The time pattern of aircraft movements can be observed from Table 5, which shows the number of landings and take-offs in each hour in the week starting April 11, 1988. From the whole-day point of view, the arrival frequency is almost constantly high throughout the week, ranging from seventy-nine on Wednesday to eighty-seven on Monday. A similar observation may be made about departures, the busiest days being Tuesday and Sunday (eighty-five departures) and the lightest day being Wednesday (seventy-nine departures). If one looks at the hourly figures a different result is found. One observes large variations in frequencies. For arrivals, the peak hours are 12:00 to 15:00. On average, thirty arrivals fall within these three hours every day, equivalent to 37% of daily arrivals. During the peak hours, on average, there is one arrival every six minutes. It is clear that the airport is operating at full capacity during these three hours.

In fact, an average of one arrival every six minutes over a three-hour period conceals the true extent of the congestion. The actual "bunching" of arrivals is even more serious. For example, in the hour 14:01 to 15:00 on Tuesday, there are fifteen arrivals; during the same hour on Sunday, there are thirteen arrivals. It is not hard to imagine a tired and frustrated passenger having to queue up for immigration clearance, baggage claim, customs

Table 5
Kai Tak Airport Timetable of Scheduled Flights
(April 11 - April 17, 1988)

	Mon		Tue		Wed		Thu		Fri		Sat		Sun		Total	
	A	D	A	D	A	D	A	D	A	D	A	D	A	D	A	D
8:00 — 9:00	6	4	3	3	1	3	3	3	1	4	3	3	2	3	19	23
9:01 — 10:00	2	8	1	8	3	4	2	7	3	5	2	7	2	6	15	45
10:00 — 11:00	5	5	5	5	5	6	4	6	5	6	4	6	5	5	33	39
11:01 — 12:00	7	5	4	5	7	4	6	4	5	4	6	4	6	4	41	30
12:01 — 13:00	9	7	10	7	10	8	12	6	9	7	11	7	10	8	71	50
13:01 — 14:00	10	10	9	10	8	10	6	13	9	8	8	13	8	9	58	73
14:01 — 15:00	8	7	15	7	9	7	11	6	11	8	11	6	13	7	78	48
15:01 — 16:00	2	11	3	13	3	9	2	9	4	12	2	9	3	12	19	75
16:01 — 17:00	1	3	1	7	2	5	2	4	1	7	2	4	2	6	11	36
17:01 — 18:00	8	0	3	0	4	2	6	2	6	1	6	2	5	0	38	7
18:01 — 19:00	6	8	6	3	5	5	8	6	7	5	8	6	7	5	47	38
19:01 — 20:00	6	2	5	2	7	3	6	3	5	2	7	3	5	4	41	19
20:01 — 21:00	6	5	5	5	6	6	5	6	6	6	5	6	8	8	41	42
21:01 — 22:00	7	4	8	4	6	3	6	3	7	4	6	4	6	3	46	25
22:01 — 23:00	4	4	3	6	3	3	4	4	3	4	4	4	2	4	23	29
23:01 — 24:00	0	1	1	0	0	1	0	0	0	1	1	0	0	1	2	4
TOTAL	87	84	82	85	79	79	83	82	82	84	86	84	84	85	583	583

A: Arrival
D: Departure

Source: South China Morning Post (April 11 - April 17, 1988)

checking and taxis together with three thousand other passengers if he or she is unfortunately caught in the "peak of peaks". By contrast the "light" hours are a world apart. For example, there is only one or at most two arrivals in the hour 16:01 to 17:00. Even in the hours 9:01 to 10:00 and 15:01 to 16:00, there are at most three or four arrivals. During these hours, the airport is under-utilized. Just like the Mass Transit Railway, ferries and buses, the airport suffers from a "peak-load" problem. The crux of the problem is that the user, in this case the airline, is not made to pay a price compatible with the scarcity value of landing time (with direct implications for the utilization of airport facilities) during peak hours.

This argument applies equally well to the departures situation. The two peak hours seem to be separately 13:01 to 14:00 and 15:01 to 16:00. On average, there is a plane departing every 5.7 minutes during either of these two hours—causing considerable congestion.

If we combine the arrival and departure situations, we see that 12:01 to 15:00 are the busiest three hours for the airport. While the design of the airport effectively separates the incoming and outgoing passenger traffic, three consecutive hours with more than seventeen air movements in each hour inevitably lead to considerable stress among air traffic controllers, airline personnel, immigration officers and to motor traffic congestion and car parking space shortage.

Worth special emphasis is the safety aspect. The airport operates all movements on a single runway. This means that when one plane is landing, there cannot be another plane landing or taking off. During the peak hours with seventeen movements an hour, even if the even spacing of plane movements could be attained, there would be one landing or take-off every 3.5 minutes. The stress on the air traffic control personnel is thus easy to perceive. Considering that stress causes errors and given the awkward city-centre location of the airport, it is in everybody's interest (as opposed to only the passengers' interests) to ease the congestion of air traffic.

Auctioning Landing Time Slots

As previously mentioned, in the last two decades, passenger traffic through the airport has been growing at an annual rate of 11.6%. There is reason to believe that the growth trend will continue. The Southeast Asian region plus Japan, Taiwan and Korea will continue to increase their share of the global income and their wealth relative to Europe and North America. The opening of China will continue to attract China-bound and China-originated traffic to Hong Kong. Also, the economic growth of Hong Kong will generate more traffic. If the government liberalized the airline industry, traffic would grow even faster. Unless a constraint such as limited airport capacity is allowed to hinder traffic growth, Hong Kong will in future maintain its position as a major hub in the region, alongside Tokyo, Bangkok and Singapore. From the long-term point of view, it seems inevitable that it will be necessary to expand the physical capacity of the airport. It may turn out that constructing a new airport to replace Kai Tak is the best strategy considering the limited expansion potential of the Kai Tak site. But the worrisome question is, no matter what the government decides to do, the physical airport capacity cannot be expanded in time to cope with increased traffic in the near future. It is against this background that it is worth considering auctioning landing time slots to ease congestion. It will be seen that the auctioning scheme is equally applicable to a future airport.

As we have seen, the landing and take-off frequencies at Kai Tak Airport are quite uneven over the day. Different landing and take-off times are not equally attractive to the airlines. The present situation is that during peak hours, facilities are over-utilized but during light hours, under-utilized. Although the airport administration imposes a Peak Movement Surcharge on peak hour traffic in addition to the normal landing fee, the price variation is insufficient to prevent uneven utilization. A better way to introduce optimal price differentials to solve the problem is by auctioning the time slots, i.e., assigning a time slot to the airline that bids the highest price for it. While the principle of auction is simple, implementation requires careful consideration. When the auctioning scheme is first introduced, it would be best to concentrate on either landings or take-offs. If an airline had to secure both landing and take-off time slots by bidding, it would face a formidable task in valuing different time slots, as the desired take-off time would depend very much on the landing time which the airline could secure only by outbidding other airlines. Because of this, the airline might not be able to react quickly enough in an auction. In deciding between auctioning landing slots or take-off slots, then landing slot auctioning should be tried first. Other supporting reasons include the fact that incoming passengers are causing more congestion and are often more impatient. For simplicity, we shall concentrate on the auctioning of landing time slots. The auctioning of take-off slots could be deferred until sufficient experience has been accumulated.

While the auctioning scheme allocates airport resources efficiently, it does reduce airline profits. Those airlines which occupy the prime time slots would see their profits being reduced. Therefore, they would strongly oppose auctioning. This is where liberalization enters the picture. Under liberalization, airlines would have even more freedom to set airfares. The cost of securing the popular time slots would be reflected in higher airfares. Those who are unwilling to pay high airfares can choose flights arriving at less popular hours. Notice that consumers would have a wider variety of choices than is now available.

To implement the auctioning scheme, several questions must be addressed:

(1) How many slots should there be in an hour?
(2) What kind of auction should be used?
(3) Should there be a reserve price?
(4) How frequently should the auction be held?
(5) Could time slots be sold or exchanged after auction?
(6) How should delayed flights be treated?

These issues are taken up in turn below.

(i) The Number of Slots per Hour

Under the auctioning scheme, the number of landings that the airport can handle depends on the number of opening hours and the number of landings allowed in an hour, i.e. the number of slots per hour.

Kai Tak Airport is situated in the middle of the densely populated Kowloon City district so noise pollution is always a problem. It is now only open for fifteen hours from 8:00 to approximately 23:00. Actually, the midnight and early morning curfew may not impose serious constraints on airport capacity because few passengers would want to land in these hours and so the airlines cater to their preferences. In addition, the airport has to be closed for cleaning, maintenance, etc. So, suppose we keep the number of operation hours to the existing fifteen hours per day.

If we desire an absolutely even distribution of landings over the fifteen hours, then only six scheduled passenger flight landings would be necessary in one hour because, at the moment, the number of scheduled passenger flight landings does not exceed ninety in any single day. The scheme need not, however, be very rigid. Uniformity is not essential. It may even be impossible in view of curfew hours at other airports.

When the airlines bid for the landing slots, their valuations of them would be revealed. We would probably see that the slots in the peak hours command very high prices. At present, airlines are forced to charge the same price for the same route, they cannot compete with each other in terms of price. Therefore they try to attract passengers by offering better service. Landing at a convenient time is one important service.[3] Therefore if it turned out that demand for landing slots during, say, 12:00 to 15:00 was very high, the airport administration might consider allowing

---

3 Because of regulation, even non-price competition is severely limited. Good flight schedules are therefore highly valued.

more landings in that hour, which may still be within the comfortable limits. On the other hand, fewer landings between 22:00 and 23:00 might be considered desirable because it would be less disturbing to nearby residents. The auctioning scheme is compatible with such arrangements.

The reader may ask whether one could not simply restrict the number of landings per hour to achieve the desired distribution of landings without resorting to auctioning. In theory it is possible, but in practice it is not. Without auctioning, there would be no equitable way to move certain flights away from the peak hours. Those airlines whose flights were allowed to retain their peak-hour landing slots would enjoy what is known as a "monopoly rent" forever because competition in the use of their slots would now be barred by the administration. Charges of favouritism and unfairness would surely be raised against the government. A further advantage of auctioning would be the revelation of the worth of landing slots to airlines. This valuable information would help the government in judging the economic case for capacity expansion or a new airport.

(ii) The Kind of Auction

Four main kinds of auction are currently in use in the sale of commodities: the English auction, the Dutch auction, the sealed-bid first-price auction and the sealed-bid second-price auction. The English auction is by far the most common method. Bidders make their bids orally and the commodity is given to the highest bidder, who pays the amount he bids. The Dutch auction involves the auctioneer dropping the price gradually until a bidder stops him. The winner pays the last price. In the sealed-bid auctions, the bidders tender their bids privately. The first-price auction gives the commodity to the highest bidder, who pays the price he bids. The second-price auction gives the commodity to the highest bidder, who pays the price that the second highest bidder bids.[4]

---

[4] For a survey of auctioning literature, see McAfee and McMillan (1987).

In the case of the auction of landing slots, the two sealed-bid auctions would not be suitable. If there were six hundred time slots to be auctioned and an airline could only make, say, seven landings, it could bid sensibly only if the six hundred slots were auctioned one by one. In addition the costs of administering and participating in such a sealed-bid auction are very high, hence not advisable. Both English and Dutch auctions are applicable but, since a Dutch auction requires a high opening price, the level of which is unknown to the airport administration due to lack of experience, the English auction is favoured. Furthermore, in the beginning, airlines would watch how others bid in order to help them decide on the true value in an English auction. Such information would not be available under the Dutch auction.

When the auction took place, the time slots would be up for sale sequentially. Airlines would then make bids for a time slot and the last bidder, in other words, the highest bidder would get the time slot. Then another time slot would be brought up and so on.

A well-known problem with English auctions, especially for the revenue maximizing auctioneer, is collusion, i.e. bidders agree prior to an auction not to bid the true value and share the surplus that results from the winner obtaining the commodity at a price much lower than its true value to him. In order to succeed, collusion must take place among all the high bidders because one high bidder who does not join in the collusion will force the truly highest bidder to bid close to the true value, thus breaking the collusion. At the moment, there are some thirty international airlines serving flights to Hong Kong. The probability of all or even most of them colluding is extremely small.

(iii) Reserve Price

At present, each landing requires a landing fee and also a peak movement surcharge if the landing takes place in busy hours. These levies could be abolished under the auctioning scheme and be replaced by a reserve price, or base price, for each time slot at the auction. The average landing fee in 1986/87 was roughly

HK$6,500. Therefore, when the auctioning scheme is newly in troduced, it would be advisable to set a somewhat similar reserve price for each time slot. This would ensure that sufficient revenue would be generated by the auction to cover the overhead costs of the airport. As experience accumulates, the reserve price could be adjusted appropriately. However, the peak movement surcharge should not be incorporated into the reserve price of any slot. This surcharge is an ad hoc way to reflect the scarcity value of landing time in peak hours. Under the auctioning scheme, the scarcity value of landing time would be reflected by the bidding price. The surcharge would therefore be redundant.

(iv) The Frequency of Auctions

The frequency of holding auctions is worth consideration because a balance has to be struck between minimizing costs to airlines and the airport administration on one hand, and enabling the airlines to plan and publicize revised schedules on the other.

Since the auctioning scheme would be new to the airlines and the airport administration, some familiarization period would be required in the beginning. As experience was acquired, the costs of running and participating in an auction would mainly be labour costs. Actually, only the slots in peak hours would involve active competitive bidding. The slots in light hours could be quickly assigned.

One means of holding the auction that is worth considering is computer networking. Because of the need for computerized bookings, all airlines have computer terminals. Auctioning would only require one terminal for the airport administration, who would act as the auctioneer, and one terminal for each Hong Kong-serving airline—all connected together to form a network. The auctioneer could signal which slot was currently being auctioned and each airline could make a bid via its terminal. Each bid would then be shown on all terminals although the airline that made the bid should be known only to the auctioneer. Since an airline would not know which airline was making a bid or the slot assignment situation at any time, the possibility of collusion and the scope of strategic bidding would be greatly reduced. While there are costs associated with conducting frequent auctions and should therefore be avoided, airlines might wish to make route changes from time to time. Under the auctioning scheme, an airline that was assigned a slot would have to pay the bidding price even if no landing was subsequently made in actual fact. Therefore it would seem undesirable to tie the airlines down to their landing slots too rigidly for too long. Moreover, the scheme should not prohibit new flights from developing just because the desired landing slots had been assigned. The airlines introducing new flights could compete for landing slots with the airlines running "existing" flights. On the other hand, airlines need to know the slots they are assigned before making flight plans. Frequent flight rescheduling is somewhat costly.

Participation costs, flexibility to allow for route changes, and costs of rescheduling flights are among the major factors that determine the suitable frequency of holding auctions. The airport administration can choose the optimal frequency of auctions, although auctions once every six months for the six-month period one year ahead may be tried out at the beginning.

(v) Resale of Landing Slots

The right to a landing slot is an asset to an airline. It allows exclusive use of the airport during the specified time. If landing slots were transferable then changes in the pattern of passenger demand can be readily accommodated, including seasonal patterns. An airline that wishes to reduce some flights, increase others or just change landing times to suit passengers would be able to secure them from other airlines. Transferable slots would ensure that landing slots were used by the airlines that valued them most. In other words, the allocation of slots would always be economically efficient. Of course, by selling a slot, an airline might reap a windfall gain. This is of course the risk-taker's gain and exists because auctions could not be held frequently enough to ensure landing time changes necessitated by all intended flight changes were quickly accommodated. Therefore, transferable slots would have an efficiency advantage not attainable otherwise.

While transferable slots are desirable they also introduce some complications. The airport administration would incur additional costs in monitoring such transfers. Some airlines might wish to bid for more slots than what they actually need for their planned flights. They may hold them just to deprive other airlines from having access to prime time landing slots, although their ability and willingness to do this could be quite limited in view of the enormous costs required. Nevertheless, if it were to occur it would be a waste of resources. Traffic growth might also be jeopardized. Speculation might also take place, however, this is not a problem in itself. Not all the consequences can be predicted at this stage, but the primary advantage of having auctions should not be obscured as a result. Initially when the auctioning scheme was first introduced, slots could be made nontransferable. To prevent wasteful hoarding, the administration might even restrict the number of slots to be held by an airline to the number of landings that it could make. As experience accumulated, the more efficient option of transferability could then be considered.

(vi) Delayed Flights

Flight delays are inevitable and usually unintentional. Bad weather and mechanical failure are the most common causes. Passengers usually blame delays on the airlines, which, in order to maintain their reputation, try hard to avoid them. Under the auctioning scheme, there would be a possibility that an airline that failed to secure a good landing time might deliberately delay departure in order to land at a more favorable time. If this were practised regularly enough, even passengers might treat it as normal, which would then be unfair to the airlines that paid a high price to land at that time.

In view of these possibilities, a penalty charge for delays would be necessary. In practice, whether a delay is intentional or not may be hard to judge. Unintentional delays are difficult to deter using a penalty charge because of their very nature. In any case, passenger complaints act as a deterrent. Therefore it is mainly intentional delays that could be inhibited by better regulation. A progressive scale of penalty charge could be adopted. The penalty charge payable would increase with the number of delays that had occurred with an airline. This should eliminate the incentive for an airline to delay their flights regularly to take advantage of better landing times. The maximum penalty charge should be approximately the difference between the prices of the dearest and cheapest landing slots.

A related question is how accurate landing time could possibly be in practice, particularly that of long-haul flights. For example, it might be perfectly acceptable for a flight from London to arrive twenty minutes early or late. The airport administration would need to work out a tolerance range for acceptable landing time deviations.

Some Queries

Some queries might be raised about the proposed auctioning scheme. In anticipation of these queries, the following attempts to provide some answers.

(1) Would landing slot auctioning lead to some giant airlines dominating the airport?

At present, the number of flights into the airport is fixed. Each airline can only serve as many flights as they are licensed to. Therefore, restricting the number of landing slots held by an airline to the number of flights that it is licensed to offer would prevent the airline from dominating the airport. Under liberalization, each airline is still not allowed to hold more slots than its flights require. An airline's number of flights to Hong Kong is constrained by fleet size. Moreover, even if allowed, excessive acquisition of landing slots would not turn out to be profitable. While the airline that monopolizes the airport for some time might be seen as offering good service to the consumers, the bidding mechanism implies the slots could only be secured by bidding exorbitant prices. Furthermore, the incentive to monopolize landing slots could be eliminated by having the airport administration stipulate that a landing slot assigned but not subsequently used by an airline would be reassigned to another airline.

(2) Would airlines bid for the early morning landing slots if other airports do not at present allow take-offs that are early enough to allow the planes to land in those slots?

If there were little competition for the early morning landing slots, the auction prices for them would be relatively low. Airlines would like to take advantage of them. One way is to reschedule the long-haul flights to land in these slots. Another way is to persuade or pay other airports to allow early take-offs.

(3) Would it be unfair to let the auction price apply to all plane types without regard for their capacities?

It is true that a Boeing 747 plane which carries 400 passengers can bid more for a landing slot and cause more congestion at the terminal than a DC10 plane which carries 230 passengers. To be an effective hub, an airport requires a mixture of long-haul and short-haul air services. Many airlines that fly short-haul routes tend to use small planes. An airport that sought to maximize its revenues would seek to arrange its auctioning scheme for various flights so as to optimize the mix of plane sizes.

(4) Would airlines find it difficult to plan flight schedules under the auctioning scheme?

Clearly, an airline cannot plan its flight schedule before it gets to know the slot assignment situation. To deal with this problem, the slot auction should take place well in advance of the date when the slot assignment takes effect. In this way, airlines could plan and announce their flight schedules well in advance. Moreover, if the industry were liberalized and airlines had more freedom in setting airfares, the airlines would know how much to charge for a flight that would land in a particular slot.

Conclusion

Kai Tak Airport suffers from congestion. A close look at the airport timetable shows that landings and take-offs are distributed quite unevenly over the operating hours. As a solution to ease congestion, an auctioning scheme is proposed which spaces out landings to achieve a more efficient utilization pattern for the airport. A similar scheme for the auctioning of take-off time slots could be considered subsequently as experience accumulates. It should be emphasized that it is auctioning of landing time slots that is proposed, not landing rights. Landing rights are still determined through bilateral air services agreements.

While the principle of the scheme is simple, its implementation would require careful planning. The airport administration could decide on the optimal number of landings to be allowed in each hour. Uniformity is not essential. There could be more landings during daytime and fewer at night.

While different types of auction are in use, the English auction is considered most suitable. A reserve price which would equal the present landing fee is advisable in the beginning to cover overhead costs. The optimal frequency of auctions can be determined by the airport administration in light of various administrative and technical costs.

While a time slot won at an auction would be an asset, to avoid unnecessary management complications in the beginning, it is recommended that slots be non-transferable between airlines. In addition, airlines might not be allowed to hold more landing time slots than are necessary to land their planes.

A question that arises in practice is whether airlines should be penalized for landing time deviations, and if so, by how much. The airport administration should decide a tolerance time interval with penalties for failure to land within the allocated time interval. To deter recurrent delays, a progressive penalty charge scale might be adopted.

The auctioning scheme is equally applicable to Kai Tak Airport and any other airport where there is scarcity of landing time slots.

5   Conclusion

Two interconnected schemes are proposed to solve the two main problems confronting the international airline industry today, namely, rigid regulations and airport congestion.

To liberalize the international airline industry it is not enough to merely demonstrate the costs and benefits of a liberalized environment because of vested interests in the present system. Multilateral negotiations to open up the markets are unlikely to succeed as witnessed in the Chicago Convention of 1944. Some countries would have to be encouraged to liberalize. It is proposed that Hong Kong take the initiative to bilaterally liberalize with other countries according to a scheme called the Sequential Bilateral Liberalization scheme. In Phase One of this scheme, Hong Kong would seek to negotiate the equivalent of a bilateral free trade agreement with the U.S., Japan, Taiwan, Thailand, Singapore, the U.K., Australia and Malaysia. This would permit airlines in these countries an unlimited right to land in Hong Kong, and vice versa. Phase Two would involve bilateral liberalization with other countries that are geographically close to the eight countries. Phase Three would involve liberalization among all these countries. Each phase generates incentives for countries to proceed into the next phase. In this sense it is a sequential process. Hong Kong's major task is to initiate Phase One. It is anticipated that, after liberalization, traffic volume would sharply increase. Therefore, it would be essential for the airport administration to adopt an auctioning scheme to handle the increased traffic.

At present, Hong Kong's Kai Tak Airport is already quite congested. It is suggested that the airport should auction off landing time slots in order to more evenly distribute landings and passenger flow over the day. The proceeds from the auction could be used to maintain and upgrade airport facilities. As experience accumulated, the auctioning of take-off slots could be undertaken as well. If the airport administration adopted this policy, the need for a new airport may become less urgent in the short run, although in the long run, the physical capacity would become a binding constraint on the volume of traffic that could be handled. It is proposed that an English auction with reserve price should be adopted. The option of transfer of landing time slot rights after auction, while desirable, need not be allowed initially.

In connection with the liberalization issue is the problem of granting to Hong Kong's new airline, Dragonair, the right to operate certain air routes. Under the present regulatory system a route granted to Dragonair would probably mean a route lost to Cathay Pacific.[1] The issue becomes largely a matter of how to share a pie of fixed size between two parties. Any decision can have only a profit redistribution effect on the shareholders of Cathay Pacific and Dragonair. In a regulated international setting, the two airlines have no room to compete fairly. Therefore, the government must negotiate with other countries for more route grants. The best way to solve this problem is to negotiate for bilateral free markets. In this case, Cathay Pacific and Dragonair could both expand their networks. They would then not only have to compete against each other, but against airlines of the other countries as well.

There are those who worry about the fortunes of the two Hong Kong airlines under liberalization. Although it is difficult to make accurate forecasts at this stage, there is good reason to believe that both airlines would do as well, and probably do bet-

---

[1] On the contrary, Dragonair claimed that in one case, although it was allowed to land in a foreign country, its route application was turned down by the government.

ter, under liberalization. Cathay Pacific is an efficient and fast-growing airline that has won worldwide acclaim recently, while Dragonair has been incurring losses due to insufficient air routes. In Phase One of the SBL scheme, both airlines should gain in the U.S., Japan, Taiwan and U.K. markets, while Cathay Pacific might lose slightly in the Thailand, Singapore, Australia and Malaysia markets. As Phase Two came into operation, both airlines would experience vast expansion in flight opportunities and by the time Phase Three took effect, the worldwide traffic volume would have increased dramatically. Both Cathay Pacific and Dragonair would have plenty of opportunity for growth.

Hong Kong would also benefit enormously from liberalization. As the number of flights between Hong Kong and other countries increased, business in hotels, restaurants, retail firms, means of transportation, and other tourism-related industries would boom. Moreover, the increased flights would also mean greater travelling convenience, so Hong Kong, already a busy hub, would become even more accessible. This would bring indirect benefits to trade-related industries and financial industries as well. The same could be said for the entire Pacific region.

To the traveller, liberalization would bring lower airfares, more price-quality combinations, higher flight frequency and better managed airlines. In 1987, 1,386,484 Hong Kong residents travelled abroad (excluding to China). It follows that even a modest reduction in airfares would bring enormous benefits to the travelling public. Benefits also accrue to travellers in other countries who fly to Hong Kong and the region.

The eight countries which the Hong Kong Government could approach in Phase One should have good reasons to welcome such an initiative. Their airlines and consumers would gain under bilateral liberalization with Hong Kong. Other countries such as Canada, South Korea, India and European countries other than the U.K., which might be unwilling to liberalize in the beginning, would, over time, rethink their stand when they saw the benefits that liberalization brought and the losses they incurred for not joining in.

In conclusion, there is much to be gained from liberalizing the international airline industry. Air routes should be opened up to enable airlines to compete freely; however, they should be charged for the use of the airport to avoid congestion. The present situation is far from this ideal. The Hong Kong Government is in a position to play a major role in rectifying some of these problems, which would benefit the people of Hong Kong and in the rest of the world as well.

Bibliography

1. *ABC World Airways Guide (1988)*: Reed Telepublishing Ltd.
2. Bailey, Elizabeth E. (1981): "Contestability and the Design of Regulatory and Antitrust Policy", *American Economic Review Papers and Proceedings*, Vol. 71, No. 2, pp. 178-183.
3. Bailey, Elizabeth E., Graham, David R., and Kaplan, David P. (1985): *Deregulating the Airlines*, MIT Press, Cambridge, Massachusetts.
4. Bandow, Dong (1987): "Airlines : Prime Target for Privatization", *Journal of Economic Growth*, Vol. 2, pp. 23-30.
5. Baumol, William J., and Willig, Robert D. (1981): "Fixed Costs, Sunk Costs, Entry Barriers and Sustainability of Monopoly", *Quarterly Journal of Economics*, Vol. 95, No. 2, pp. 405-431.
6. Caves, Douglas W., Christensen, Lauritis R., and Tretheway, Michael W. (1981): "U.S. Trunk Air Carriers, 1972-1977 : A Multilateral Comparison of Total Factor Productivity", *Productivity Measurement in Regulated Industries*, Academic Press, New York, pp. 47-76.
7. Caves, Douglas W., Christensen, Laurits R., and Tretheway, Michael W. (1984): "Economics of Density versus Economics of Scale : Why Trunk and Local Airlines Costs Differ", *Rand Journal of Economics*, Vol. 15, No.4, pp. 471-489.
8. Chuang, Richard Y. (1972): *The International Air Transport Association*, A.W. Sijthoff, Leiden.
9. Demsetz, Harold (1968): "Why Regulate Utilities?", *Journal of Law and Economics*, Vol. 11, No. 1, pp. 55-65.

10. *Economist* (1988): "Aviation Brief : It's Getting Mighty Crowded", February 27, pp. 64-65.

11. *Economist* (1988): "And Nowhere to Land", February 27, 1988, pp. 11-12.

12. Faulhaber, Gerald R. (1975): "Cross Subsidization : Pricing in Public Enterprises", *American Economic Review*, Vol. 65, No. 5, pp. 966-977.

13. Fisher, Franklin M. (1987): "Pan American to United : the Pacific Division Transfer Case", *Rand Journal of Economics*, Vol. 18, No. 4, pp. 492-508.

14. Graham, David R., Kaplan, Daniel P., and Sibley, David S. (1983): "Efficiency and Competition in the Airline Industry", *Bell Journal of Economics*, Vol. 14, No. 1, Spring 1983, pp. 118-138.

15. Heilbronn, Gary H. (1988): "The Changing Face of Hong Kong's International Air Transport Relations", *Journal of International Law*, Vol. 20, No. 1, pp. 195-224.

16. Hong Kong Tourist Association (1988): *Overseas Travel by Hong Kong Residents 1987*, Hong Kong.

17. Hong Kong Tourist Association (1987): *Hong Kong Tourist Association Annual Report, 1985/86*, Hong Kong.

18. Kahn, Alfred E. (1988): "Surprises of Airline Deregulation", *American Economic Review, Papers and Proceedings*, Vol. 78, No. 2, pp. 316-322.

19. Keeler, Theodore E. (1972): "Airline Regulation and Market Performance", *Bell Journal of Economics*, Vol. 3, No. 2, pp. 399-424.

20. McAfee, R. Preston, and McMillan, John (1987): "Auctions and Bidding", *Journal of Economic Literature*, Vol. 25, No. 2, pp. 699-738.

21. Morrison, Steven A.,and Winston, Clifford (1985): "Intercity Transportation Route Structures under Deregulation : Some Assessments Motivated by the Airline Experience", *American Economic Review, Papers and Proceedings*, Vol. 75, No. 2, pp. 57-61.

22. Panzar, John C., and Willig, Robert D.(1977): "Free Entry and the Sustainability of Natural Monopoly", *Bell Journal of Economics*, Vol. 8, No. 1, pp. 1-22.

23. Posner, Richard A. (1974): "Theories of Economic Regulation", *Bell Journal of Economics*, Vol. 5, No. 2, pp. 335-358.

24. Pryke, Richard (1987): *Competition Among International Airlines*, Thames Essays No.46, Trade Policy Research Centre, London.

25. Hong Kong Government, Civil Aviation Department (1988): *Report on Civil Aviation Hong Kong 1986-87*, Hong Kong Government Printer.

26. Rosenberg, Arne (1970): *Air Travel Within Europe*, The National Swedish Consumer Council, Stockholm.

27. Sawers, David (1987): *Competition in the Air*, Research Monograph No.41, Institute of Economic Affairs, London.

28. Scherer, F.M. (1980): *Industrial Market Structure and Economic Performance* Ch. 18, Rand McNally, Chicago.

29. Stigler, George J. (1974): "Free Riders and Collective Action", *Bell Journal of Economics*, Vol. 5, No. 2, pp. 359-365.

30. Straszheim, Mahlon R. (1969): *The International Airline Industry*, The Transport Research Program, Brookings Institution, Washington D.C.

31. Westlake, Michael, and Jeffries, Brian (1988): "Aviation and Aerospace '88", *Far Eastern Economic Review*, February 4, 1988, pp.39-67.

32. White, Lawrence J. (1972): "Quality Variation when Prices are Regulated", *Bell Journal of Economics*, Vol. 3, No. 2, pp. 425-436.

33. Williamson, Oliver E. (1976): "Franchise Bidding for Naturnal Monopolies in General and with respect to CATV", *Bell Journal of Economics*, Vol. 7, pp. 73-104.

34. Winston, Clifford (1981): "A Disaggregate Model of the Demand for Intercity Freight Transportation", *Econometrica*, Vol. 49, No. 4, pp. 981-1006.

35. Winston, Clifford (1985): "Conceptual Developments in the Economics of Transportation : An Interpretive Survey", *Journal of Economic Literature*, Vol. 58, No. 1, pp. 57-94.

Index